How to Homeschool Your Child
and Unlock their Genius

by

David Simon

Published by Simon Education

©David Simon 2016

All rights reserved. No part of this book should be copied in any format.

The information in this book is advisory only. The reader should consult a qualified professional for guidance on education matters. The author and publishers cannot be held responsible for actions that may be taken by the reader as a result of reliance on the information contained in this book. The information is taken entirely at the reader's own risk.

Contents

Section 1:   How to Homeschool Your Child

Section 2:   Resources

Section 3:   Understanding the Education System

Section 4:   Case Studies

Section 5|: Cultural Literacy

Section 6:   Mobile Learning and Online Education

Section 7:   Homeschool Models

Section 8:   Trends in Employment

Section 9:   Recommended Books

Section 10: Health and Learning

Section 11: Who Will Name Our Children?

Section 1: How to Homeschool Your Child

Homeschooling is when parents or guardians decide to educate their children at home, normally by themselves but increasingly with online tuition support. The Western homeschool movement was very much inspired by Rudolf Steiner (1861 – 1925) and in later years by the educationalist John Holt, author of the classic book, *How Children Fail*. In the US the number of children being homeschooled is around 2 million and in the UK it is around 150,000. With the growth of the internet and online tuition there was a big growth in this area during the mid 1990s. In addition to this, another factor that has led to this growth has been the online career, with more people able to work online from home or even run their own home based business via the internet.

Why Home School?

The reasons for parents wanting to home school their children vary with academic reasons topping the list at 48%, followed by religious/moral reasons at 30% and behavioural issues at 15%. However, in my experience with the parents I have worked with, school racism has been the main factor. Homeschooling your child requires a variety of skills and resources. For some groups homeschooling can be a combination of these issues and more. In the African-Caribbean communities of the US, 220,000 families now homeschool their children. The homeschool movement is now growing in the UK amongst African-Caribbean families.

So what steps should parents take when homeschooling their child? Simon Education has mentored many families on homeschooling and has found that the following needs to be in place, although it should be noted that there is no one best way to homeschool all children.

1. Devise a six month plan of action before the start date of your homeschooling
2. A letter of deregistration should be completed and sent to the school and local education authority in order that the child is taken off the school roll (UK).
3. Homeschool curriculum should be identified.
4. Identify out-of-home learning opportunities like museums, libraries, galleries and community projects such as an urban farm etc.
5. Homeschool teachers need to be identified and receive general training if possible. Support teachers should be identified in the event of illness of main teacher.
6. Homeschool support network should be identified or developed to ensure wider socializing for both student and parent.

7. Online homeschool support should be identified for online tuition.
8. Identify relevant homeschool resources that cater for all learning styles.
9. Devise school calendar with key Pan-African dates.
10. Devise a homeschool file which should contain:
    - Health and safety documentation and other policy documents
    - Homeschool timetable
    - Schemes of work
    - Lesson plans
    - Progress reports and assessment results
    - Learning style questionnaires
    - Learning agreement
11. Devise learning portfolio containing examples of students' work.

It should be noted that the student should also have ownership of the learning experience and be consulted at every stage. Once these basics are in place then homeschooling can be fun, exciting and extremely rewarding.

As part of our inquiry into homeschooling we need to delve into the actual journey to homeschool from a Pan-Africanist perspective as the need to homeschool is part of the reconstruction of the Pan-African family structure. It is an attempt to reconstruct the compound family, a multi-faceted family with its collective democracy, its traditional court, business activities, and its function as a family school that incorporates the parent-teacher, the classroom teacher, the community teacher, the peer-teacher and now, the digital teacher. What is the real motive to homeschool the Black child from a historical and spiritual perspective? Our journey starts with Makeda and Errol, and their son Kobi which, is presented to the reader in a story, a key component in African pedagogy.

 The Sankofa symbol reminds us of the importance of learning from the past whilst moving forward. This symbol reminds us to always be moving forward whilst returning to our roots. In our inquiry into learning the Sankofa symbol reminds us of our great system of education based on family and the need to reintroduce family learning to the community.

Makeda's Story: The Homeschooling Family

Although it seemed like an ordinary day, it wasn't despite the grey sky, the stubborn snow and racing children who ran towards the school gates as the bell rang. It had, in fact, been the day when she knew she had to stick by her decision

to make the biggest choice of her life and that was to homeschool Kobi. That morning, after she had bathed she had rubbed herself down with Shea butter and, oils and prayed in her mind, she decided to refuse to allow any hopeless thoughts to come into her head and ambush not only her dream but Kobi's too. It was as if she conducted a private ritual, a cleansing one for she saw her work to homeschool her child as some kind of stance. She stared at the big old brick building, knowing that it was soon to be the last time she  would drop him off at this tired school, with its tired teachers, tired curriculum, its tired books and tired lessons. Fortunately, she had banished all anger from her and was slowly beginning to relish the beauty and dedication of the work ahead. Yet there was a pressing urgency. She only had seven days, seven days before her homeschool was to start and she needed to discover seven angels within herself that would unlock her child's genius. Now real anxiety caught her. Just at that moment a bird began to circle above the school, a strange but almost magical bird that seemed to want her attention, calling not just her but something within her to follow it. It would have been easy for her to have ignored the bird if it had been an ordinary day, but it wasn't and so she studied its wing span, studied its flight, its spiraling then watched as her eyes blinked to keep doubt away. Suddenly the bird flew off in the distance, leaving her puzzled but increasingly anxious as to where it had gone.

By the time Makeda had started the car and began to negotiate the ill tempered traffic, she started to see the bird again. By now there was a growing feeling that it was trying to tell her something but with this realization came the thought that this was ridiculous. How could a bird that should be well on its ways to southern skies be calling her? As she drove the spiraling bird led her towards Deptford, to the market where labouring shop owners and crouched stall holders were just setting up for the day. She parked her car by the old railway arches that often acted as a hotel for the homeless. Not knowing why she kept walking even though there was now no sight of the bird but she knew that where she was at that moment was where she would discover the first of the seven angels. Unknown to her these were the same roads that the Black Victorians had walked; the streets that Oludah Equiano and Sancho had trod as abolitionist and writer, and unknown to her these same shops stood on the grounds where the Moors, who had been banished from Spain in 1492 had come to England and set up their practices as cartographers, leather specialists, needle makers and the many exquisite trades that they had brought to Spain and Europe from Africa. And she didn't know, that she walked on pavement that lay on top of cobbled Roman roads that African legions had pounded the stubborn earth flat. So all about her was a fake reality. This was why it was no ordinary day. And the shops that she walked past many times before, now seemed different. They had different windows, strange hanging signs, peculiar goods that belonged to another era in history. There were small dusty antique shops, specialist maritime shops, second hand furniture shops, run-down charity shops, pop-up shops, trendy galleries and odd shops. Finally, slightly squinting, she was drawn into one of them. It was a second-hand book shop, boxes filled with books and old magazines but one particular box stood out. Yes it was old, and worn and torn but the books seemed special as if it wouldn't open for anyone else but a particular reader. The box contained an odd collection of book. Some were on war dogs, some were on the building of early railway lines, some were on English law but there was one that appeared to be handmade. As she walked into the cluttered premises the elderly shop owner whose crinkled face blended with the antiques and crumpled crochets smiled at her. Her hand, as if guided, reached for it.

"Stubborn one that," spoke the cockney shop owner as he strained to bring out more boxes of books to the front-table where he hoped to entice passers-by. She turned it over as she examined the cover which had written on it the title Secrets of the Ethiopian Ocean. In the opening pages was a strange map of the world that had Africa at its centre and labeled India, Eastern Ethiopia, and the Atlantic Ocean, *The Oceanus Aethiopicus*. And there were faded drawings of ships with black sailors, and black kings and queens. Almost without looking at the old shopkeeper she stretched into her deep coat pocket and pulled out her purse which she opened, her eyes fixed on the map and the stories it was beginning to conjure up then gave him some money. Before he could get her change she had left the shop and was looking up in search of the bird which was flying high in the sky, almost escaping her gaze that seemed to remain with her until she found herself in her car where she eagerly began to read the slightly torn book; flicking through the pages as she discovered another passage that brought her deeper into this world of ancient African maritime adventures.

It appeared that the book was a short story book. Stories about adventures of black sailors of Kush, old Kamit and the great Phoenicians who had lived in what is known today as north Palestine. She managed to control her wayward imagination, and then began to read the first story that was called *Lesson of the Goddess.* The language was strange, formal even, yet full of poetry that brought Makeda to a place of ship building, long forgotten cartographers, brave sailors and magical storms and seas. The first story was short and mysterious. It was about a mother and her son, a sailor, in the time of Kush, a time long before the great 25th dynasty that would re-take Kamit (ancient Egypt). The young man was serving his apprenticeship as a sailor, and so had to load supplies below deck which he had to also scrub, then hoist sails and help with the ship's repairs. It was to be his last voyage before he would be considered a qualified sailor, but in truth he was sailing to seek revenge on the person who had murdered his father, so he was eager to sail with his hidden motive. The mother had watched the wind take her son away; watched the ship's sails balloon with tireless winds that had always been loyal to the great ships of Africa. Each day late in the evening as the Moon came out, the mother would sit on the beach hugging her knees waiting for the ship to return. This happened for months until one night as the angry waves slapped the beach the stubborn ship appeared again as the seas tossed it high into the air. To her it took hours to anchor, then the wait for the seas to calm in the early hours of a still morning. Eventually she saw a small boat rowing towards her as four strong but weathered men chopped the sea with their oars. She couldn't wait so she ran into the water, her sister now reaching out after her as she kicked the sea water until she got to the boat where the men with sadness in their eyes gave her the news. "Him dead! He drown in de big sea. De Great Goddess take him." She screamed so loud that civilisations of the ancient world could hear as she fell, grief stricken into her sister's arms. At this point Makeda also had tears in her eyes, but she had to read on. She stopped reading, but knew that this was no consolation for the mother, this character from the book that was now so real. She felt that there was a fight not only for the son, but his right to grow up as a man. This is what she feared for her own son, Kobi. The school was stopping him from being a man, and she didn't want the street to falsely claim this training ground for him. The same too was happening to Errol, her husband, who had to work around the clock to be that man who could provide, yet he came home defeated each day, barely listening to Makeda's talk on how the plans for the homeschool were coming on even though he knew they had to do something. The ancient story continued and saw the mother sneak out of her wooden house to the beach where she whispered to the Great Goddess of the Sea to help her find the body of her son. Almost naked, her breasts exposed and with just turquoise cloth tied around her thighs and waist, she entered the sea prepared to die if the sea was to reject her quest. She splashed and splashed, gasping for breath now regretting her foolishness but before she could become another victim, several brown skinned mermaids circled her, their braids tangling together to form a kind of raft for the mother to travel on. She held their braids tightly watching their fish-like swim slicing the water yet they didn't even appear to be breathing and their faces were one of calm. Finally, as the sea creatures glowed even more they took her to the sea palace of the Goddess of the Ethiopian Ocean. Never had the mother seen such a sight, for there before her was a brilliant white palace made of white cowry shells, gold and pearls; a magnificent palace guarded by creatures no human had ever laid eyes on before. Amidst all this the mother suddenly realised that she was now breathing under water and that the braids of the mermaids had released her as she found herself half floating half standing before the goddess who stared into her soul then spoke.

"Why have you come?" The mother swallowed hard but she was determined to speak.

"I've come to take my son's body home. The other sailors said he drowned in search of *pearls in your ocean but his body was never recovered. Please, I ask you, help me to find his* body so that I can take him home. The goddess reached down to her feet where a pinkish sea shell was placed and brought it close to her lips.

"Tell me, where does this woman's son's body lie," she whispered to the shell. Almost as if a trance she brought the shell to her ear as she combed back her long black locks and listened for the answer. The beautiful brown face of the goddess became serious which frightened the mother, causing her to take a few desperate steps towards this queen of the underworld. Just at that moment the goddess of the spectacular palace signaled for the mermaids to go, speaking to them in a language that the world would later know as the Kush script. In an instant they swam off, this time in a great hurry as if time was against them. The mother became even more anxious. The goddess opened her palm and released an oil that found its way to the mother, entering her body through the navel and calming her with a melody that helped her to relax throughout the long wait which was also short in human time. When the melody finally faded the mermaids returned, this time carrying the dead body of her son in their tangled braids.

"Heru!" She screamed, "Please live, open your eyes! Speak to me!" Again the mother was becoming distraught, her fists pounding the sea all about her. The goddess shook her head, then looked at the mother, prepared now to tell her about the laws of the Great Ethiopian Ocean.

"Your child has gone, dear mother of the land."

"No," screamed the woman who felt betrayed by the goddess.

"The only thing that can bring your son back to life is for you to piece together the child's existence before all hope of life leaves him. Your son is blind, not dead. Before you can give him life, you must give him sight. Make him see truth and he will live!" The mother shook her head as she knelt over her son's body.

"The laws of the *Ethiopian Ocean* gives power to those who obey all its rules. Go away and devote yourself to leading as good a life as you can. Do to others as you will have them do to you. Banish all evil thoughts from your mind. Care for others, especially the creatures of the sea and air. Be silent and pure when others are angry. When you have achieved all these things, come back, look into the soul of your son and ask if he wants to live again and live in accordance with the law of harmony of the ocean. The mother reluctantly left the body of her son and returned to *The Land of Kush* where she purified her life by living in accordance of these seven laws. A year later, according to what Makeda read, the mother returned, her hair now in locks and her body scented with jasmine. Before the *Great Goddess of the Ethiopian Ocean*, she looked down at her dead son and asked his spirit if he wanted to live again and live in accordance with the seven laws of the Ethiopian Ocean. But the son would not speak. He remained silent. The mother looked at the goddess as if betrayed by the instructions, but the great ruler of this underworld city offered the mother the shell which she had once consulted a year ago. The mother, holding the shell delicately, put it to her ear and listened. No one knew what the soul of the son said, but within seconds the young man had opened his eyes, choking as the mother dropped the shell, embracing him as she knelt down and cradled his head.

From that day onwards the mother and the son tried to live by the seven laws which meant they were always in harmony with the Great Ethiopian Ocean.

Makeda read and re-read the story trying her best to piece together its significance. All she knew that she was to devote herself to bringing out the greatness in her son, that she had to live by these seven laws of the *Ethiopian Ocean* and that one day the knowledge that she was to accumulate would be given to the whole world to enjoy.

Section 2: Resources

Homeschooling is about empowering the child, parent and home and such an undertaking demands powerful questions to be asked to give clarity to the whole endeavour. The questions below are some of the ones that Makeda should have asked, or will ask. These are the questions I have asked parents who have wanted to homeschool. On a practical level it prompts the homeschooling family to devise an achievable action plan, to seek further support and advice and to further strategise. In essence a think tank arises; yes, it should be called this. This think tank must be guided by various levels of thought. First we have to apply logical thinking to the undertaking and reason as to the practicality, feasibility of the homeschool operating. Next we have to inspect the undertaken holistically, looking at all the components of homeschooling in terms of family and community empowerment. Thirdly we have to inspect the 'truth' of the undertaking. We have to ask, is homeschooling in harmony with the infrastructure of Nature, that is, will the undertaking be detrimental to others.

Home School Questionnaire

General Questions

1. Why do you want to homeschool your child?
2. How does your child feel about being homeschooled?
3. Who will be homeschooling your child?
4. Have you explored all options in keeping your child in a mainstream school?
5. Have you undertaken any research into the resources and skills needed to successfully homeschool your child?

Your Skills and Training

1. Which educational philosophy will you follow in homeschooling your child? E.g., Steiner, Simon, Montessori (unitary or co-operative).
2. Have you undertaken a formal consultation on homeschooling your child?
3. Have you undertaken any formal training to become a successful parent-teacher?
4. Which curriculum will you follow? E.g., National Curriculum (UK).
5. How will you devise a workable syllabus to use on a daily basis?
6. Have you identified transferable skills that you will use to make yourself a successful parent-teacher?

Your Child

1. Does your child have any special educational needs?
2. Has your child been statemented (UK)?
3. Have you identified your child's learning style?
4. Do you know the attainment level your child was at when you withdrew them from school?
5. Do you know the attainment level your child was at when you withdrew them from school?
6. How will your child socialize with other children whilst they are being homeschooled?

Teaching and Resources

1. Do you have the necessary teaching resources to run a successful homeschool?
2. Have you identified any online teaching resources that you can access to support you in homeschooling your child?

Your Child's Homeschool Portfolio

1. Your child's portfolio and school file should consist of:
- Contents page
- Scheme of work
- Individual learning plan
- Daily timetable
- Register
- Progress report
- Examples of completed work (P)
- Reading record
- Homeschool policies

External Visits

1. How often will you visit the local library?
2. How often will you visit a museum?
3. How often will you visit a local gym/sports centre?
4. How often will you visit a theatre?
5. Exhibitions.

Continuing Professional Development

1. How will you continue to develop your skills whilst homeschooling your child?

2. Will you join any homeschooling networks in order to improve your teaching skills?

The Homeschool Curriculum

A curriculum is defined as a course offered by an institution or followed by an individual or group. A national curriculum therefore might be defined as a course that a government instructs all schools to follow and in a set manner. That is, the government determines the subjects, the assessments, the teacher training requirements and the accreditation. Of course the homeschool family should acknowledge this curriculum but they should also note its limitations and the political nature of the curriculum. I have always proposed that a second curriculum be followed that lends itself to the empowerment of the family and community. Such a strategy essentially requires a cultural base that consists of knowledge, tools and resources that have been proven to support self and community development. The aim of this cultural empowerment curriculum is to:

1) understand self and community needs;
2) help develop strategies to unlock the genius of self and community;
3) to develop institutions, centers of power and resources to help facilitate Black African community development;
4) to help build the infra-structure to enable the efficient dissemination of the curriculum to develop, adapt and empower the community;
5) to act as the key resource in the training of the key teachers;
   - the parent teacher
   - the classroom teacher
   - the community teacher
   - the peer teacher
   - the digital teacher.

When the homeschool family adopts the national curriculum, if that curriculum is politicized then they are immediately disempowered; they will probably not have any choice due to a lack of an alternative curriculum. Subjects will be delivered in chunks, assessments prescribed by people outside of the community, resources supplied by large educational suppliers whose interests are profits only and who have little interest in the community in which the resources are used. Moreover, the system of accreditation is controlled by "outsiders" who leave the homeschool family/community powerless. The Black African, regardless of where they reside has to address this issue, for even Black countries with their own education departments are subject to this same issue for they have not addressed the ownership of knowledge and the validation of their own indigenous knowledge. To achieve the above the Black African researcher has to have many skills but the main one is courage for they will have to go against their training, having graduated or been educated within the western intellectual tradition. In undertaking this important research they will not win awards, achieve academic status but they will help liberate their own minds and that of their community. Being aware of this I developed the eLearning course, entitled Global African Studies. This is the cultural base for me and the wider Black African community. The African researcher will, in their great journey, come across African sculptures, frescoes, carvings, pyramids, jewelry, all of which speaks to their spirit but they will be dumb before them for they are untrained. These artifacts and monuments speak to their spirit, though they were not told this at university or school, and are central to their knowledge base. They might find themselves in a western museum surrounded by masks that want to speak to them, telling them to live truth (Maat). Ancient books of Africa that they never knew existed, books from libraries long destroyed: African libraries Carthage said to contain over 500,000 volumes; libraries at Thebes, Jenne and Timbuktu universities and in the Moorish city of Cordova. They will hear the cries of the scribes, authors, librarians, cartographers and artists running for their lives as their libraries are burnt down and looted. Secretly, for they know that they are not supposed to have these thoughts they will wonder what happened to these great books. With tentative footsteps they will venture into the back rooms of museums where the books are now kept; they will venture to places that became translation centers so that each word from these Black African libraries could be copied and given new authors, where new universities could emerge. Little would these African researchers know that the very university that they attended was built on knowledge that their ancestors helped to create. The African cultural base needs to be restored and is central to the homeschool movement.

The homeschool movement will play its part in building a global library from which the great centers of learning can once again emerge for they are practical places focused on learning; a place where innovation, creativity and courage resides.

Homeschool Resource Table

This table should be prepared for each session to ensure that the learning caters for all students with varying learning styles and learning paces. These resources help the learning experience to be a more meaningful, effective, interesting, fun and creative.

Using visual/tactile aids is often useful in breaking up a sedentary learning experience and allowing the learner to explore a concept and encouraging kinaesthetic learning. The resources of the activity table also allow for pair and group work.

Everyday resources

Whilst it is useful to have these resources on a table to allow easy access they can of course be placed on the table(s) where the students are working. Often having the resources visible and therefore easily accessible allows for improvisation in the learning when a teacher can utilise a resource that they had not envisaged being used. It might even allow the teacher to reinforce a concept that a student might be struggling to grasp.

Resource	Function
Key Stage Primary (5 – 11yrs)	
Mathematics	
Dice & rulers	To develop counting skills
Rulers, rubbers & sharpeners	
Clocks and measuring tape	To understand time & measure
Pens and pencils	Writing and drawing
Coloured pens/crayons	Writing and drawing
Coloured paper, glue, safety scissors	Writing, drawing & arts and craft
Protractor, set square, calculator	For shape, space and measure work
English	
Picture dictionary	Developing vocabulary and spelling.
Flash cards	Developing vocabulary and spelling.
Word dominoes	Developing vocabulary and spelling.
Puzzles	To develop concentration skills, thinking skills and problem solving skills.
Science	
Science flip chart & markers	For general science teaching & drawing diagram.
Science text books	For general teaching and self study.
Cultural Literacy	cds & workbooks.
CD Player	Auditory learning, music and drama work.

How to Homeschool Your Child

Resource	Function
Key Stage Secondary (11+)/grade 5 +	
Mathematics	
Rulers	To develop counting skills
Rulers, rubbers & sharpeners	For general work
Pens and pencils	Writing and drawing
Coloured pens/crayons	Writing and drawing
Coloured paper	Writing, drawing & arts and craft
Protractor, calculator	Measuring angles and various operations
English	
Dictionary	To help develop vocabulary.
Thesaurus	To help develop vocabulary.
Word dominoes	To help develop vocabulary.
Science	
Science flip chart	For general science teaching & copying diagram.
Science	
Science textbooks	To complete science assignments.
Cultural Literacy	Workbooks, pictures, cds
CD Player	To create learning ambiance in 2nd session.
Flip chart paper	For class teaching.

Resource Design

Adinkra Symbol 	**Traditional African Writing System** Hwemudua is the symbol of examination. The journey that the child will take in completing this book will help them to develop a habit of inquiry that will in turn help them to unlock their genius. The hwedmudua symbol is here to remind both student and teacher that learning is about investigating: questioning, reading, listening, speaking and even being silent.

Below are samples of resources that we have designed to teach a range of topics:

Cultural Literacy

Cultural literacy exercises feature in the *How to Unlock Your Child's Genius* workbooks as part of the teaching of Global African Studies. The workbooks contain exercises in African culture, English, Mathematics and Science. As the workbooks are part of a family learning series then it is important that these exercises are accompanied with family learning activities for the parents/community to engage in.

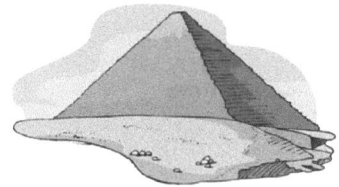

Assignment 1

Africa: Birth Place of Humanity and Civilization

Africa was once joined to the other continents of the world (during early Mesozoic era) that formed a massive continent called Pangaea.

You could put more than half of the world into Africa and still have areas left over. So we can see that Africa is not only the hottest continent in the world but one of the largest and its original inhabitants are blessed with melanin. Study the map of Africa below and undertake research to decide whether Africa is the first or second biggest continent in the world.

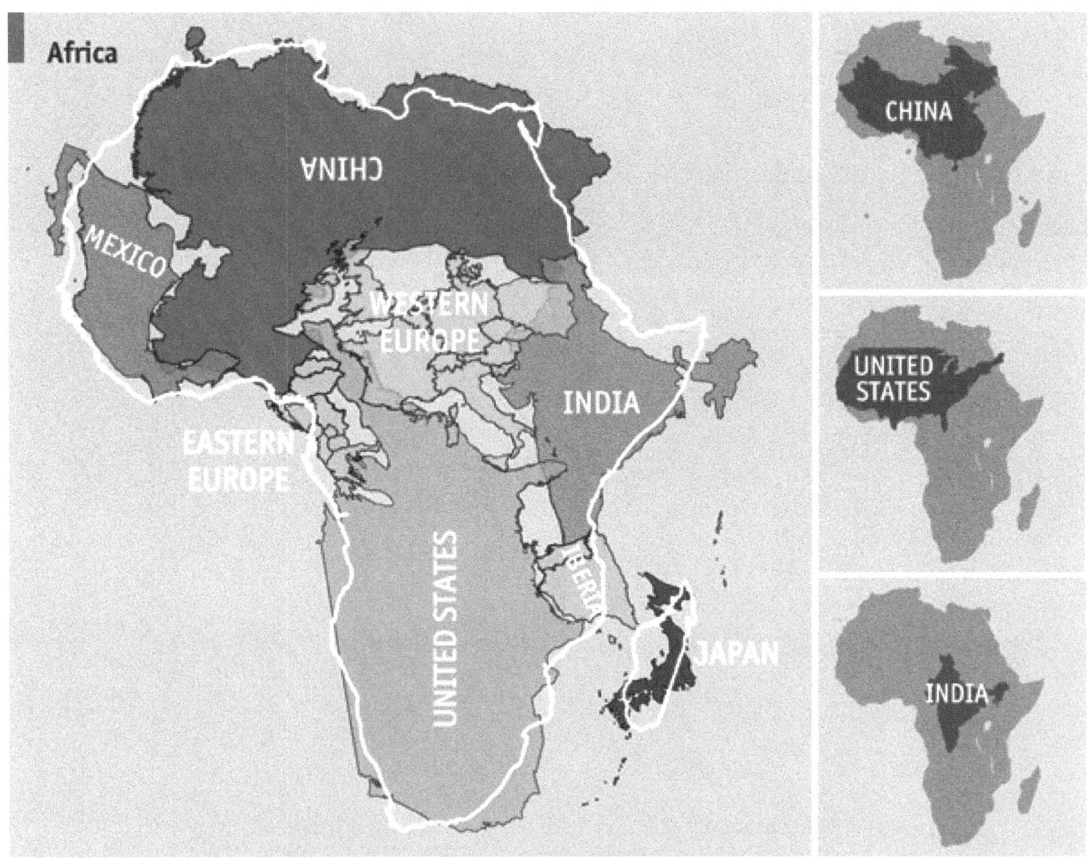

source: The Economist 2010

Task 1

Study the map of Africa below and write the names of as many African nations as you can.

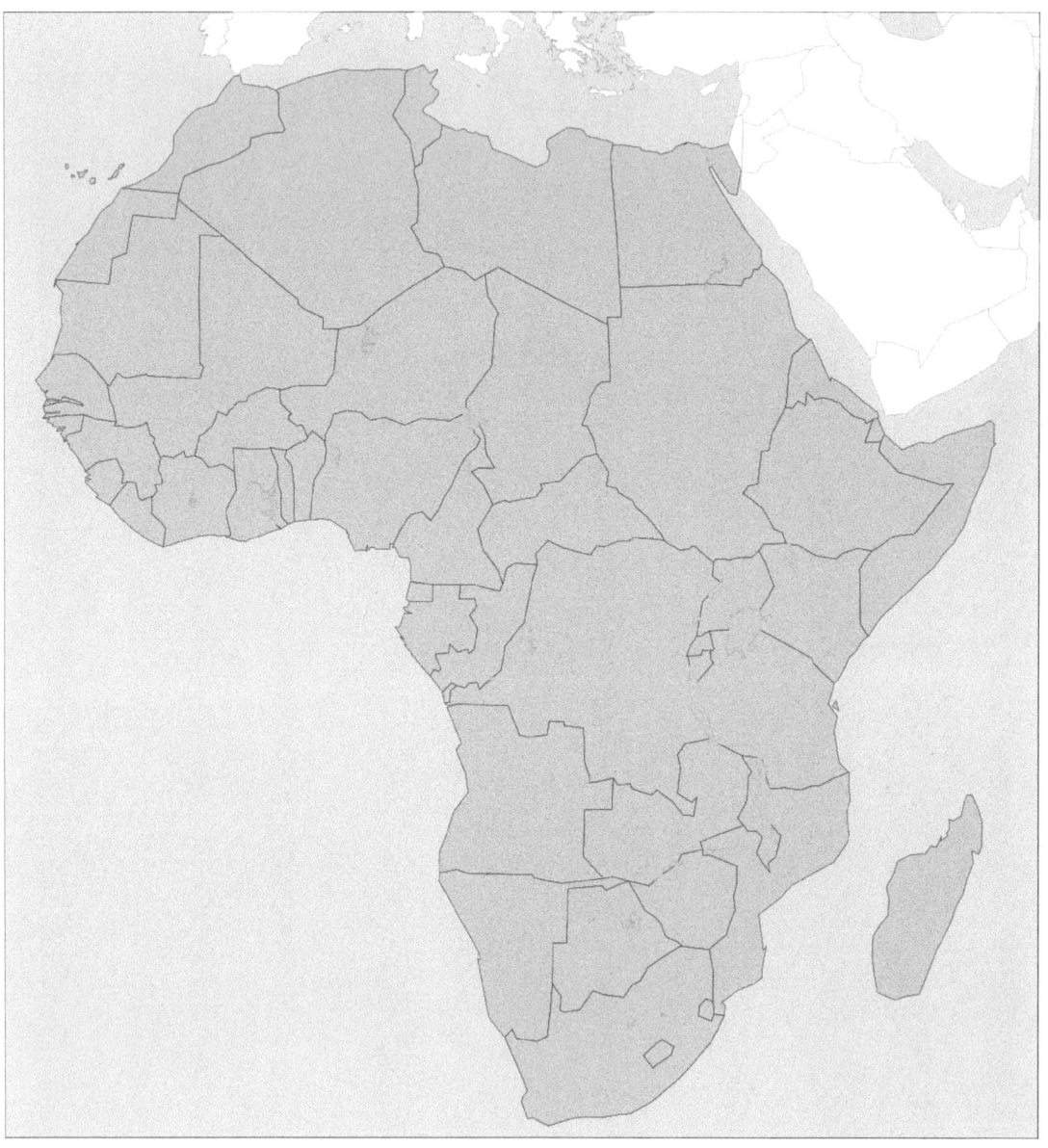

How to Homeschool Your Child

African/Ancient Egyptian Grammar

Hieroglyphics or Metu Neter as the ancient Egyptians called it was the script that was developed by the Africans of the Nile Valley civilization.

Phonograms are sound signs and ideograms are sense signs that convey their meaning pictorially. Often the ideogram follows one or more phonogram and ends the word indicating the precise meaning to be comprehended.

Study this ancient Egyptian alphabet and complete the questions below.

How to Homeschool Your Child

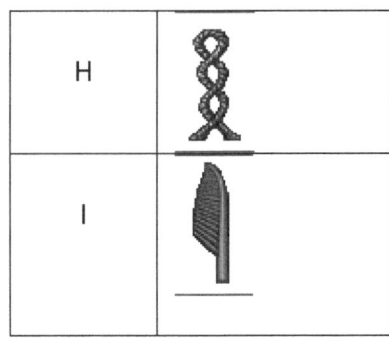
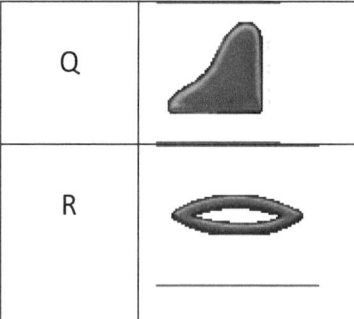
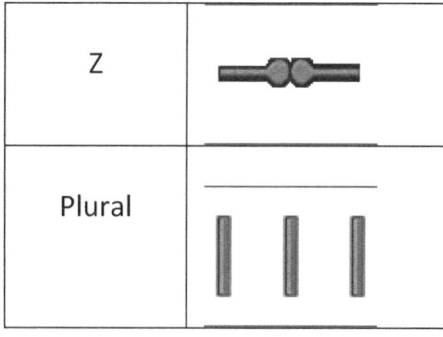

1) Spell the word **SCIENCE** using hieroglyphic symbols.

   ....

2) Draw the symbols that use birds. Why do you think birds were used as symbols?

   ....

3) If the word **MATHEMATICS** uses eight symbols, which are the hieroglyphic symbols that appear twice in the word?

   ....

4) Which are the first two hieroglyphic symbols that appear in the word **PHYSICS**?

   ....

5) Which same hieroglyphic symbols appears once in the word **BIOLOGY** and once in the word **CHEMISTRY**?

   ....

How to Homeschool Your Child

An African Cartouche

1. The Egyptians wrote the names of their kings and queens in an oval shape called a cartouche. Copy the cartouche below and using the alphabet above try and work out which famous pharaoh it shows.

 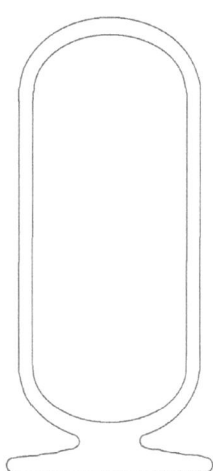

....

2. The Ancient Egyptian number system used the following symbols to indicate the various numbers. Study these symbols and write the number 1, 300,255 using hieroglyphs.

The Ancient Egyptian Number System

|	1
||	2

(spiral)	100
(lotus)	1000

21

				3
					4
						5
							6
								7
									8
										9
∩	10

(symbol)	10,000
(frog)	100,00
(figure)	1 million

....

The development of teaching and learning resources should be informed by research and monitored practice.

Section 3: Understanding the Education System

Designed to Fail: The Modern Education System

One of the only places operating largely as it did more than 50 years ago would be the local school.

RENATE NUMMELA and GEOFFEY CAINE

Making Connections

When I started Simon Education Saturday schools, I did not realise at the time that one of the many skills it would require was that of *listening*. Over the last twenty-nine years I have listened to 15000 families; parents, mostly mothers, complain about poor schooling, or the labeling attached to their child, like that of dyslexia. I have listened to them complain about not being able to get their child into the school of their choice. When I have listened to the children they complain about bullying, about boredom in school, about the regime of testing, assessments and exams, and when I listen to teachers they complain about endless paperwork, the sterile curriculum, or poor school leadership, and they complain about student behaviour and lack of parental support. Somewhere amidst this are clues to the solutions. Whether we look at the micro or macro situation with regard to education, both are alarming. In 2007 in the UK the statistics that are usually quoted regarding the education of African-Caribbean children are: African-Caribbean children are three times more likely to be excluded, only 31% of African-Caribbean achieve GCSE grades A- C, and only 23% of Black Caribbean pupils achieve A-C grades GCSE grades as compared to the national average of 40% (Reach Report, 2007). In 2013/14 there is a major change in these figures with African-Caribbean children 2.9% below the national average of 56% with 53.1 % achieving 5 A-C GCSE grades (dept for Education UK 2015). Unfortunately when Black youth are mentioned the following statistics are closely followed by the mention of black youths involved in the criminal justice system, gun and gang crime, which are often linked to poor education, lack of opportunity and other issues. Again, data around this further failing in the community is of concern:

- Black people are six times more likely than White people to be stopped and searched with arrests being 3.4 times that of white people.

- Black youths are over represented as youth offenders accounting for 6% whilst only being 3% of the 10 – 17 years old in England and Wales
- Black young men in UK are 5.5 times more likely to be a victim of homicide than White people.
(Reach Report, 2007)

A report card produced by The Africa-America Institute (2015) provides us with further evidence of the need to find both micro and macro solutions to the educational needs of African worldwide. The report highlights:

- 38 million African children were not in school in 2012 and half of these will never enter a school of any sort.
- After qualifying for secondary education 36% of children will not be accommodated.
- Teacher/pupil ratio in Africa is 42:1. This statistic (2012) has not changed since 1999.
- 40 million more youths are projected to drop out of school in the next decade.

Few question as to how we have arrived at this situation. These statistics have arisen from an *industrial model* of education that started in late 19th and early 20th century in America and Europe. It is time for us to investigate an alternative education system that might be closer, and more natural, to us than we think. The nuts and bolts of schooling in UK, Caribbean, Africa and elsewhere normally consists of 'armies' of school administrators, curricular, teachers and learners in a place we call school. The parents, the children and teachers are all struggling with this outdated model. This was brought home to me when, in 2005, I delivered a teacher training workshop in Grenada. The teachers seemed to be in despair, not knowing what was going wrong, or who to turn to. They believed that they needed more resources, more trainers from UK, more support. They complained of not being valued and the status of the profession. The following year, 2006, I again delivered a teacher training workshop in Ghana, on my book *How to Unlock Your Child's Genius*. Again the teachers made complaints; echoes of Grenada, and again they wanted more solutions from the west. By the end of both workshops I knew that what they needed was a new philosophy of education. At no time did I get the impression that they questioned this old industrial model of education they were trying their best to work with.

The Present Model of Education

Type of Education	Venue	Educators	Assessment Methodology	Parental Involvement

Early Years	Nursery/ School	Nursery Nurses	Exams & tests	Limited
Primary	School	Teachers	Exams & tests	Limited
Secondary	School	Teachers	Exams, tests & portfolio	Very limited
Tertiary	College	Lecturers	Exams, tests & portfolio	Extremely Limited

The above model is what most industrialised nations use and Third World nations often copy. We have seen that it does not work. Typically the features of this model are:

- Children grouped by age
- Curriculum broken into subjects
- Syllabuses delivered by teachers who are trained only to deliver this model
- Pupils tested by paper-based exams and tests
- Compulsory national curriculum that has mathematics, English and science as its core subjects
- Government body assigned to monitor school performance
- Little formal parental or community involvement

In *The Learning Revolution* (2001) Vos and Dryden, demonstrate that the learning revolution needed for the 21st century will be radically different to this old model that has spread across the world and is accepted as the norm. They go as far as to quote Dr. Willard Daggett (Director of International Centre for Leadership and Education):

The world our kids are growing up in is changing four times faster than our schools.

Writers on the Left like Michael W. Apple (*Education and Power*, 1995) say that school is simply a place where the government makes children learn technical and administrative knowledge but does not educate them to address inequalities in society.

Five education movements which have consistently challenged this modern schooling are:

1. **Education Research** – Michael W. Apple (*Education and Power*, 1995), John Taylor Gatto (The Underground History of American Education, 2001) & Amos Wilson (*Awakening the Natural Genius of Black Children*). These authors demonstrated the built in inequalities of the education system in terms of class and race; that the real function of school is to prepare children by social class for industry. They question the myth that school is a level playing field, that education allows for social mobility and they question the very idea of a 'good education'.
2. **The Home School Movement** – Here children are taught in their homes by their parents. John Holt (*How Children Fail*, 1984) has advocated that parents should be able to educate their children at home because school makes children fail; the child is bored, afraid and confused.
3. **The Supplementary School Movement** – Here children go along to a small centre and are taught the basics as well as some form of cultural studies. This movement as we know it in the UK started in 1965 to address the growing concerns of the African-Caribbean community on the underachievement of their children in British Schools. Later the Rampton (1981) and Swann (1985) reports would further identify the causes of underachievement as being the British school system. Closely linked to this movement is Bernard Coard's book, *How the West Indian Child Is Made Educational Sub-Normal in the British School System* (1971). This pamphlet articulated what the community knew was happening, in that there was widespread low expectation of white teachers towards African-Caribbean children.
4. **The Charter School Movement,** - Non-sectarian public schools that offer greater innovation in teaching practices; give access to high quality education, work with a less restrictive curriculum and provide choice to parents. This movement began in 1970s in New England and has spread throughout the US (40 states). Some of the aims of these schools are that they encourage greater parental and community involvement and are better able to serve a special/local population and create new professional opportunities for teachers.
5. **Independent Schools**, - these schools have been set up by individuals or groups outside of the public education system, and have often had a particular mission and vision to educate children based on a particular religious approach, or an education philosophy like that of the Steiner-Waldorf schools (based on the work of Rudolf Steiner, 1861-1925), and the Montessori schools (based on the work of Dr Maria Montessori, 1870 - 1952).

It is the grassroots supplementary education movement that I belong to and the online education movement. In 1987 I founded Simon Education Saturday Schools, a social enterprise, providing additional learning support to African-Caribbean children and young people. There were some 3000 of these schools, though figures differ drastically, and it is here that I, along with others, have investigated an alternative education system that places the family at the centre of the learning experience. However, let us first look at the existing model and even search out its origins.

The traditional education system is obsolete.

Richard L. Measelle and Morton Egol

Transforming Education: Breakthrough Quality at Lower Cost

The Origins of the Modern Education System

The modern mass schooling, that was to spread to Africa and the Caribbean during slavery and colonial times, was a synthesis of many movements and approaches to education but one essentially of servitude for the various powerful elites of the West. These influences were:

- **The Prussian influence**. According to the educationalist John Taylor Gatto, it was in the 1820s when the Prussian influence started and when the American mass school movement got under way between 1905 – 1915 which was influenced by the work of Alexander Inglis's book, *Principles of Secondary Education* (1918). This advocated the constant testing and the dividing of children into groups by age, by subject which would result in them being unable to organise collectively as adults. This Prussian schooling system had undermined the democratic developments amongst the working people of Prussia. The big industrialists of the day, Andrew Carnegie and John D. Rockefeller also funded schools that worked along these lines as they wanted a compliant workforce.
    - **The Industrial Revolution**. In England, in 1870 the Elementary Education Act was passed which signaled compulsory education and all the education acts that followed were for the benefit of industry. Education was now industrialised, meeting the needs of England's industrial revolution that had taken place in the second half of the 18th century. A new kind of worker was required and education was to now create it.
    - **The Church and Missionary Education**. In Britain the Church of England and the Roman Catholic Church played a crucial role in providing schooling for the working classes, as they wanted them to be able to read the bible and therefore to convert to their religious practice. Missionary education both in England and the colonies had a three-fold purpose; firstly to spread the gospel, secondly to educate Christian converts to hold positions of power and thirdly, they proclaimed, that of so-called philanthropy. Their curriculum was simple; they taught religious instruction and basic skills.

    - **Professionalising Teaching**. Until 1890s the churches monopolized the provision of teacher training through the denominational colleges with the Church of England being the most important education pressure group in England. In the US, after 1918, as State schools slowly replaced private ones resulting in men leaving the profession, women, who were paid considerably less, replaced them, but now had lower status. In Britain, teacher training colleges were created to train teachers to teach the children 'of the workers' the basics. There was also a power shift with school boards and local education authorities being made up of local businessmen and a new educational bureaucracy appeared of people who knew little about education. In addition, a powerful industry around educational resources began to emerge. Teachers were trained to expect all children of the same age to be at the same standard, achieve the same results and be taught in the same way. In *Why Children Can't Read*, Diane McGuinness writes on the new school system and the de-skilling of the teacher:

> The influence of business was seen in the parallels with the newly emerging assembly-line models of industry. Schools were organised along the lines of a factory. In the US, children like battery chickens, were marshaled through 'grades', neatly sorted by age. The teacher (the factory foreman) conducted classes from the front of the room and had little opportunity to work individually with the children in her class. (p.117)

It was these influences, with their many shortcomings, that have shaped the modern schooling system. In 1979 when Maurice Bishop came to power in Grenada in 1979, one of the main thrusts of the revolution was to reform education as the inherited former colony had only 30% of its elementary teachers trained and only 7% of its secondary teachers trained. His government started Grenada's grassroots literacy program. They attempted to reform the curriculum, make the education system more efficient and provide better teacher training. They tried not to limit education to the classroom and were even advised by the Brazilian educationalist Paulo Friere. What we began to see in Grenada was a former colony trying to rid itself from this old 'industrial model' of education. The revolution of Maurice Bishop, that was eventually defeated with the American invasion of 1983, simply looked for solutions.

The Alternative Education System

The alternative education system and the solutions to the widespread crisis in global education that has its roots in this *old industrial* education system will be shaped by developing a flexible and accessible education system that can seriously address the most important issues of the day such as poverty, war, environmental damage, hunger, illiteracy, health etc. At Simon Education we have advocated the mobilisation of the community; that is, the creation of five groups of teachers:

1. **The classroom teacher**, – with greater engagement with the communities from which the pupils originate from.
2. **The parent-teacher**, – trained in developing the holistic development of the child/young person. Trained in parent-teacher programmes like Simon Education's *How to Unlock Your Child's Genius*: an eleven step parent-teacher course that gives parents the skills in

knowledge in delivering an education and empowerment curriculum like diet and learning, emotional and financial literacy, creative learning, reading and mathematics as well as learning about learning.
3. *The community-teacher*, – artists, community workers, health workers who operate in the community. Here, they must also operate from this same curriculum, providing specialist and vocational education with perhaps an even greater emphasis on community development.
4. *The peer-teacher,* - the peer teacher is the student-teacher who is still receiving their education but might be slightly older than those they teach but have the advantage in that other students can relate to them and they can act as a possible role models.
5. *The virtual-teacher*, - this virtual teacher is developing with ever greater sophistication. They operate online in the virtual space and are accessible 24/7; can mark books, lesson plan; feedback to students and parents and operate easily in several languages. They can adopt increasingly more sophisticated learning styles, and learning paces and be consistent in their delivery.

These three groups of teachers will operate in three types of 'classrooms' which might even be interchangeable. These three 'classrooms' are:

- **School classrooms**, - that will include teaching resources that also come from the cultures of the families from which the pupils come from, thereby giving them ownership of the learning experience.
- **Parent classrooms**, - typically this will be the home, but can also extend to the local library, local museum, family holiday and cultural event. Here the parent-teacher uses the home, community and local resources as the classroom, whilst also accessing other parent-teachers and community-teachers. A Network is established that sees them using their skills as mentors, life-coaches and learning facilitators.
- **Community-classrooms**, - that will include places of worship (churches, mosques, temples), youth centres/projects, community centres, rites of passage programmes, the workplace; essentially the world is the classroom.
- **Peer classrooms** - can be in the formal classroom, at home or in a suitable community space where non-academic learning might occur.
- **Virtual classroom** – a highly resourced digital space that is always accessible, low cost and adaptable.

The above initiatives will create a true learning community which will allow all institutions to work collectively to create a learning network that has a progressive curriculum as it is centered on family development. This is in opposition to the old industrial education model system that is degenerative (as the earlier statistics demonstrate) and focuses on limited technical administrative skills for short-term economic gains at the expense of the environment, family and community.

If we do not seek an alternative education system then we will have failed societies where only small elites live in affluence as in the case of the West. Statistics on the failure of the education system to deliver real social mobility and address inequalities in society reveal:

- **The unemployment gap** – 19 million people cannot find work in the West.
- **The poverty gap** – 27 million Americans are now living in poverty, and 40% are children
- **The education gap** – More than half America's young people leave school without the foundation needed to hold a good job.
- **The violence trap** – 270,000 American children carry guns to school.
- **The wealth gap** – 20% of Americans earn 80% of the country's annual income.

Source: *The Learning Revolution* by Gordon Dryden and Dr. Jeannette Vos (2001)

Humanising the Curriculum

For all these initiatives to happen we need a curriculum (what has to be taught) that is agreed by the communities that it is going to be delivered to and by. Its main features must be:

- A family-centered curriculum that has as its main focus the building and strengthening of family.
- A culture-centered curriculum that sees culture as an education resource; that sees culture as long established examples of good practice consisting of indigenous knowledge systems (IKS).
- A flexible and accessible curriculum that acknowledges its delivery by a diverse grouping of teachers and educators.
- A curriculum that promotes thinking skills and is organic in that it allows for its own review and transformation by the people it is delivered to and by.
- A curriculum that starts from birth (even pre-birth) to death and places as much importance on academic excellence as community and personal development.

I personally do not believe this revolution in education will initially come from governments, but instead, the very communities where the longstanding inadequacies of this 'industrial' education model have caused most damage. It will come from: independent researchers; the students; the parents that are forced to home-school because their child has been excluded, and the parent who cannot get their child into a good local school; the church or mosque leader who responds to the growing complaints from the parents in their congregation about the poor educational performance of their child, educational researchers: and the supplementary movement. It will come from the educational pioneers that it produces.

Governments of Africa, the Caribbean and the rest of the Diaspora have the option to continue to follow this old industrial education system or to be visionary, to be brave and adopt an education philosophy and system for the 21st century that will impact on all areas of society and lead to true, real and lasting development. These are the concerns of Makeda and Errol, and millions of families and teachers around the world, but so few have the opportunity and time to conduct hours of inquiry into this continuing crisis. Yet Makeda's spirit does. It is not a word we hear used in education, and this absence is what compounds the crisis for the Black family. Indigenous African Knowledge systems, African cosmology which is concerned with the cultivation of the human being is ignored, and banned from all the above classrooms, yet here is where the answers lie. These terms are still nouns to categorise a vast technology of practical and philosophical knowledge Black Africans have amassed on human anatomy and learning (yoga), on imagery and the brain in their writing systems (Metu Neter), on the movement of celestial bodies and radiation in African Astrology, in science and technology in their systems (computational thinking). All of these are excluded, and when the Black child is excluded from the formal school, it is the final exclusion that culminates in total exclusion of Black African genius. This is what Makeda faces; why Errol is out of the house trying to prove to himself in a world where he, the Black man, is under such vicious attack. He should have a key input in the establishing of the homeschool; what happened to his schooling that has left him lacking the resources of leadership, and so he has to fend for money by working two jobs. In truth, menial jobs that can no way unlock his genius, and help him to play an essential role in unlocking those of his son and family. As for Makeda, she continues her inquiry in her child's education by reading this obscure book with its ancient maps of Africa, and African civilizations and places that conjure tales and myths as she attempts to build her homeschool.

Makeda's Story: Sankofa

The book was determined that no one would read it until night came, which, when it happened was accompanied by a thoughtful moon. This time there was no Sankofa bird in the sky, no drifting clouds or a tingling in her spine. But the book was ready to be read and the pages almost seemed to open by itself, drawing Makeda in as the storyteller of ancient times began to tell its tale in Makeda's mind. The story started with a shocking scene. There in the opening paragraph of this fresh new episode was the mother, still distraught as she bathed the eyes of her son. He was blind. Totally blind! Makeda shook her head, not wanting to believe that another curse had fallen on the family. Before her eyes began to crawl over the old typed letters she prayed a little, prayed that her homeschool would be a success but the scene of the mother and the blind son called her. She saw them on the morning beach, the waves trying to help ease the mother's pain. Yet there was hope, the Goddess of the Ocean Ethiopia had again consulted the shell, listened to the voice that came to it and it had said, "If you want the boy to see he must find his father; this search will give him true vision, and he will see again." As the mother poured clean water into the mouth of her blind child that had been brought back to life by the goddess, the mother herself whispered to her son. "I will find your father. One day you will see again." The son raised himself up and tried to stop the mother from leaving him, but she walked quickly back into the ocean, this time knowing that she could negotiate its many worlds. The son raised himself up from the sand but his mother was now gone, gone in search of his father who'd been killed in a battle several years earlier. For a moment he was lost, lost and helpless but he stood up on his feet and shouted:

"Sankofa, come quickly. Come!" From nowhere the great bird flew down, its wingspan majestic as it glided through the air before landing by the weak feet of Heru. Immediately he grabbed the tough feathers of this great bird and boarded it like a jockey, clutching it tightly as he again shouted: "Take me into the future for I must know what will happen if I don't find my father and regain my sight." The bird soared into the morning air, its wings beating hard, its chest proud and strong. As the almost magical bird and young man flew into the future they went through different time zones, times that saw the Blacks of the earth living without the guidance of Ausar, without the wisdom of this great African king, and they saw their being defeated, fighting gallantly but facing defeat as others came to steal the minerals, great diamonds and priceless gold. Of course he couldn't see these tragic scenes with his normal eyes but sensed what was happening through the eyes of Sanokfa. And then finally, the awesome bird stopped, for there before them were the big brutal slave ships, full of traumatized human cargo, full of women, and children and beaten men. They saw great wars, brave wars of

Africans fighting back; women warriors banished from the pages of history; great African kings who would become generals and fight back, weak African kings and queens who were duped, bribed and murdered as the secret plots to enslave Blacks in every part of the world continued. They heard the screams of little African boys shouting as Arab men chained them and marched them across the Sahara then castrated those that survived; dragged their mothers into filthy harems as the men were speared, clutching the last remnants of their spiritual science before sacred shrines. And they saw crouched European men drawing up new maps of Africa. Heru shouted for Sankofa to return, to fly back to ancient Kush. When they returned to the beach, Heru dropped on the wet sand, gasping for he now knew what would happen to the Blacks if they did not rediscover *The Way of Ausar*, the great Black god. They would worship others, they would fall, be enslaved, hate their own history. Their great civilizations would be wiped from the history books, and their children educated to be dumb. As for the mother, her journey continued into the deep sea where she came across the demons of the underworld who tried to trick her as she sought Ausar, her murdered husband. In her path, as she searched for him were three headed creatures that no human had seen before, but the mother kept going in this underworld until she slowly found the dismembered pieces of the body of Ausar. Although she was distraught like any wife would be, she gallantly carried on until she held all the pieces of his body and returned to the land where her son waited for her, his mind still enraged from the scenes of his blindness. Suddenly Makeda woke up. She had fallen asleep, yet she had somehow continued to read as she slept. "And the mother. Did she find Ausar?" she thought to herself.

The next morning Makeda lay in bed still thinking about the story and deciding right there that she was going to be like the mother and son and be the most courageous homeschool teacher she could be, and that meant starting a genuine search for Ausar within herself. There was something about the mother's quest that made her feel guilty. So deep was the mother's search for her husband Ausar that it made Makeda feel as if she should somehow save Errol, her husband who she simply watched each day; watched as he ate, went to work then returned less of a man than when he left. She began to wonder if her homeschooling would help to piece together his manhood. Offer him a role of teaching his own son how to be a man whom the wider world denied him. She didn't know how but she began to feel the tears on her cheek.

How to Homeschool Your Child

Section 4: Case Studies

Home Learning Profile

This home learning profile is designed to indicate to the parent-teacher the possible areas that they need to focus on in order to raise the educational achievement of their child. Once they have completed the questionnaire then they might wish to focus on the areas where they have answered no.

1. Does your child have a space in the home where they can routinely study?	Yes	No
2. Do you have educational resources in the home to support your child's learning?	Yes	No
3. Are you following a particular home learning curriculum?	Yes	No
4. Do you routinely motivate your child through praise, earned rewards or any other method?	Yes	No
5. Are you able to access support for your child's home learning (beside your child's school)?	Yes	No
6. Do you regularly access cultural activities that help your child to have a positive identity?	Yes	No
7. Do you have a positive relationship with your child's school or college?	Yes	No
8. Do you undertake any kind of research into how to support your child's learning?	Yes	No
9. Have you set any learning goals for your child?	Yes	No
10. Have you attended a course for parents (such as *How to Unlock Your Child's Genius*) to develop your skills as a parent-teacher or learning mentor?	Yes	No

Case Study 1

One Thursday evening a call came through on my mobile from a mother who had attended one of my workshops and who now informed me that she was homeschooling her son. Her story was unusual as she had withdrawn her son from an expensive private school and now the son was at home alone with no educational provision in place to meet his needs. Just from our initial conversation I could see that she had an alternative lifestyle which seemed to also make the prospect of homeschooling her son appealing. However, this romanticism was now being confronted with harsh realities. It was late September. Her son's friends had all gone back to school from the summer vacation and her son, though not wanting to attend mainstream school, wasn't receiving any form of engaging learning.

On my first visit I had the son complete an initial assessment which showed that he was way below the national level for a child of his age. The mother seemed shocked by this news especially as she had been paying such high school fees to the private school. As for the child he was mature, keen on homeschooling but wanted an engaging education provision that had a timetable which he could adhere to. He was a young teenager who wanted to go to university and be successful in life. Above all he was a teenager with artistic talents and therefore wanted to pursue his dance and drama.

The day after our meeting I sat at my computer and prepared a timetable suited to his needs. I also gave a few introductory lessons and identified a local school where the son could sit his exams, once he had registered with the exam board. I then created a kind of homeschool network for the family so that they knew which websites they could use to access certain information and even meeting up with other homeschooling families. Both the mother and father were receptive to the home study timetable which quickly saw the son excel in all subjects. It seemed that school had held him back or that he wasn't suited to the school's sometimes regimented and sedentary style of learning, especially as his preferred learning style was partly that of self-directed learning. However the biggest plus for the teenager was the richness of the home. He was growing up in a home where there was entrepreneurship, art and care. Perhaps his parents had not thought through all the demands of homeschooling but it seemed to work out best for the son in the end. For many families who enter into homeschooling naively, it sometimes does not have such a happy ending.

What should also be noted is the urge to homeschool. This family was also wanting to reconstruct the family, whether this was conscious or not. The homeschool movement is part of this re-construction of the African family. There is a simple choice for Black African families in the Diaspora; the nuclear family or the compound family with its variety of kin relations and systems; a family structure with its roots in the African family system that afforded women-educators greater rights. With homeschool and home tuition services that I run the women are very much the educational instigators of education initiatives within the home. Both by instinct and intelligence they attempt to develop the home as a centre of learning and enterprise but often lack formal community support. The women's group, the church, the mosque, the traditional place of worship can sometimes provide a little support but specialist knowledge on "formal" Africentric education is often lacking. Their only option is to recreate the compound homeschool which they did with the African man centuries earlier. This, I believe is what the homeschool movement is ultimately trying to do. Such a brave pursuit needs a team, a group informed with an understanding of the compound family in its various forms, using African Indigenous Knowledge, as a system of self-cultivation and motivation. In recreating the co-operative homeschool they move away from European individualism.

Case Study 2

Selma comes across as an angry parent, but she is not really angry as such, but deeply resentful at the school that she has had to withdraw her child from. There were issues of bullying towards her child from other children that she claimed the school failed to address. There were issues of not being listened to, of her child being labeled when, according to her, there was a child of great talent waiting to be unveiled. And this anger is what greeted me when she phoned me to see what help I could offer. At first I had to listen to her complaints as to how she thought the school system had failed her child. I had to wait for her annoyance to give way to tears. I have learnt over the last twenty-nine years to simply listen to the parent; let them speak, for beyond the anger, beyond the tears is usually a talented parent-teacher, but for many parent-teachers they start from a position of disempowerment. Unfortunately for many they have had to hurry into homeschooling as a last resort. Most of the families that have come to me have not come from middle-class backgrounds where they might have been a tradition of homeschooling, but they have arrived at homeschooling in a state of panic and have therefore had to hurriedly discover this world of learning. It is here that they belatedly find out that education is compulsory but school is not. This was the point that this particular mother and her husband had arrived at.

In the weeks that followed, Selma and the father, told me about their son. He was a bright boy in many ways but you could see that his inquisitiveness and high energy would get him into trouble in a normal school environment. The mother was scared because the street and its world of gangs were beginning to attract her son's attention even though he was only eleven years old. I could immediately see that homeschool would not engage him enough unless there was some high energy aspect to it so I recommended he join a martial arts club which the parents agreed to try and which he later excelled in. Though I only had a brief meeting with the boy I knew him inside out because for the many years I taught in Brixton, teaching young teenagers who had to negotiate schooling - that sometimes didn't have high expectations of them; yet many of these young boys succeeded because vocational education within a further education environment suited them. They could link education and a job with their lives and it was this route that saw a few eventually go to university.

I put together a homeschool program and suggested services, websites, family support and our parent-teacher training. I knew that if their homeschooling was to be successful then a key aspect of this was whether the mother and father could calm their anger and attend to their own hidden feelings of guilt, and to an extent they did. They acquired new skills and above all a new mindset, a new awareness. The young boy was homeschooled for a while before returning to mainstream school but the experience had somehow empowered the parents and strengthened the learning that goes on in the home. This family had learnt that they could not trust their child's education to the school system alone. They became more proactive and in the process, more empowered. This empowerment was something they had not expected. In fact, my own observation when I used to teach full-time was that the Black teacher often become disillusioned with teaching but could not articulate it other than saying there was too much paperwork. I always suspected a deeper reason. This suspicion would be fuelled even more when I would meet them years later and when I enquired as to what they were doing they would tell me that they had changed careers, or at least pursuing a career in nutritional medicine, or healing, or training to be an acupuncturist. It was almost as if working as a trained teacher in the Western system had de-skilled them not simply of a range of skills, but deskilled and impoverished them spiritually. That is, working in "mainstream" education their training wasn't designed to give them the skills to cultivate the holistic intelligence of the student, but to prepare the student for a mundane and sterile existence working for an industry and global financial system that impoverished their race. This family had tasted power but it was not sustained as there was no global Black African infrastructure to harness this power.

Makeda's Story: The Search for the Seven Teachers

The laughter, the stares and gossip followed her and Kobi to school and back when she walked through the old school gates having offered a fake smile to the lollipop lady. At first she had searched the internet, then the library, then the old bookshops again for the curriculum that she knew she needed. Her great adventure to homeschool was now just five days away and she had no books, no syllabus, no curriculum and when she looked up into the grey sky there was only betrayal, for there was no bird circling above her head. A little defeated she prepared dinner, talked with Kobi, pretended to be still excited about homeschooling him and even bought reading books to give him the impression that she had everything organized. After he had gone to bed, she sat at the kitchen table, closed her eyes and put her palms over her face in the hope that an answer would appear. After some time she went to comb back her lock with her fingers when there before her was the book, open on the third chapter. She picked it up then prepared to read with a little frown.

The opening chapter was long. It meandered then eventually arrived at the stage where the son, still determined to search for his father was being led by his mother who held his arm for he was blind yet so determined to find the killers of his father. The mother, though loyal to him was scared as any mother would be for he was about to set off on another journey, this time through time to discover the consequence of the killing of Ausar.

"Sankofa, come and be my eyes." From nowhere the great bird descended from the sky, its flight majestic and full of power that had to be respected. Makeda almost expected to read on and find a mother with tears in her eyes, but this mother was herself a great fighter and whilst she worried for her son she knew he had to continue the search, so she stepped back, closed her eyes and began to sing a song to the Great African Spirit. The son grabbed a handful of feathers of the bird, and then mounted it. Sankofa flapped its wings, looked back then forward and with a mighty effort took off high into the sky as it flew into the future. All the son could feel were great gusts of air threatening to throw him over but he held on tightly. He didn't know it for he couldn't see, but as he travelled there were horrific images of war, famine, desperate migration and for many poor souls, death. The essence of the situation spoke to his soul. "Go down Sankofa, fly to the teacher." Below was a scene of carnage. Houses were being burnt, people brutally murdered, citizens of this unknown African city fleeing with what they could gather, fleeing to the interior of Africa amidst the screams. Those that fought were being killed, butchered. Great African books burnt or stolen, soon to be put on ships and taken to a museums, secret libraries. Priceless treasures were looted but worst than this, great teachers persecuted and tortured. One of these lay amongst the smoldering timbers of his house where the bodies of his family lay. He was dying and breathing his last breaths. Sankofa flew down beside him, landing on the ashes and flickering wood. The son dismounted then knelt beside the dying teacher. The young man wiped the sweat from the brow of the old man.

"Finally you have come." The words from the scribe surprised the son, as he thought he hadn't enough strength to speak.

"Are you one of the seven teachers?" The old man choked a little before speaking.

"I am the last. They have all been killed. Search for Ausar, and bring the great curriculum back to our people or they will be lost forever." Heru wanted more guidance but the teacher was weak. He knew that he had one last question to ask.

"Where do I find Ausar?" By now the eyes of the old man was closing as death approached but he managed to open them one last time.

"Just live, live the great life." Slowly the old man raised his hand and there was a beating heart and a feather that he offered to Heru. The old man's head fell to the side. He was dead. Heru took the heart and feather, at first not knowing what to do with it and then pushed it deep into his chest. The pain was excruciating, but he kept pushing it until it entered his body. When the pain died he raised his head and picked up the feather that had fallen beside him. At first he didn't know what to do with the feather but decided to tuck it into his locks. Heru mounted Sankofa and flew back in time, back to where he knew his devoted mother waited.

Makeda closed the book and stared at the cover now, for the first time, wanting to find Ausar herself, wanting to find the Curriculum of Ausar and become who would unlock her child's genius.

Section 5: Cultural Literacy

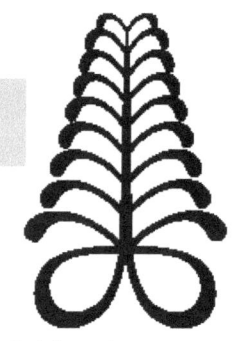

Twelve Week Reading Schedule

The suggested reading schedule below has been designed to provide your child with a variety of reading books that will develop their love for reading and allow them to explore the world of books and learning. The various book types that I have suggested are simply suggestions and in negotiation with the child the parent-teacher/teacher can devise a different reading schedule but regular reading must be undertaken.

Reading should be more than just about literacy in the narrow sense of just phonemes although this is important. For the Black child emphasis has to be placed on images and their representation, or is so often the case, their omission. In order for their talents to blossom and for them to have a love for reading, for learning and most importantly, for creating then a number of strategies have to be introduced. We might consider the first to be that of storytelling. They should be read a whole variety of stories that include the crick-crack riddles, the Anansi stories of logic and illogic, myths based on cosmology and their scientific narratives, quizzes and adventure stories. They should have the opportunity to learn the real art of writing; of writing calligraphy, the world of Metu Neter (hieroglyphs). This is what Heru of the magical story that Makeda is reading saw being destroyed. Children should be made aware that they have a great literary heritage that has seen African people invent many writing systems that include:

Scripts	Country of Origin
The Merotic script	Sudan
Ge'ez, Coptic, Sabaean	Ethiopia
Egyptian script/ Metu Neter	Kush & Ancient Egypt
The Afaan Oromo script	Liberia
Bassa script	Sierra Leone
Mende script	Sierra Leone
Nsibidi script	West/Central Africa
Edo/Benin script	Nigeria
Tifinagh script	Southern Algeria/Libya
Bamun script	Cameroon
Kukakui script	Sierrra Leone
N'Ko script	Guniea
Mandombe script	Congo

Besides these we might also include the Adinkra symbols and many other secret scripts that Africans developed, often after invasion in order to keep their indigenous knowledge. When we look at these writing systems we find phonograms, imagery, colour, extensive alphabets supported by community literacy traditions of praise songs, griots, counting games, performance poetry and call-and-response, clapping or mental arithmetic skills. This array of art forms, artistic expressions and scientific illustrations can only be delivered by teams of teachers that I outlined earlier who all adhere to a common great curriculum. This curriculum comes from the cosmology of the people themselves. It has not been imposed on them by a government who simply represent the interests of a few industrialists, but it has come from generations and generations of excellence in community and self development. When the African child is read to they develop critical thinking; when they play counting games like oware which is in truth a binary computer, they develop computational thinking skills of understanding problems, designing sustainable solutions whilst addressing apparent uncertainty/chaos. What they have to be made aware of and what is in fact going on is community education that is owned by the community and this collective effort is to: record data/knowledge, communicate this data/knowledge, store and distribute this data and allow all to have access to it at key times in the year. When a community is disempowered and therefore deskilled, then educational underperformance is likely in some instances. The answer to educational and community achievement lies with the community themselves.

How to Homeschool Your Child

Here are some writing systems that the African child should be introduced to at an early age.

Study Skills: The Hieroglyphic/African Writing System

A		J		S	
B		K		T	
C		L		U	
D		M		V	
E		N		W	
F		O		X	
G		P		Y	
H		Q		Z	
I		R		Plural	

African/Ancient Egyptian Grammar

Phonograms are sound signs and ideograms are sense signs that convey their meaning pictorially.

Often the ideogram follows one or more phonogram and ends the word indicating the precise meaning to be comprehended.

Questions on thinking skills

1. Here is the hieroglyph for **father**. Identify the phonograms and the ideogram. Use the hieroglyphic alphabet above to help you.

2. Here is the hieroglyphic word for **mother**. Identify the phonograms (letters/alphabet) and the ideograms (pictures). Use the hieroglyphic alphabet above to help you.

3. Here is the hieroglyphic word for **love**. Identify the phonograms (letters/alphabet) and the ideograms (pictures). Use the hieroglyphic alphabet above to help you.

4. Conduct research into the 25th Dynasty of ancient Egypt and write a short paragraph about them. Write some biographical notes on the king Piankhi.

Bantu Writing System

As an exercise the homeschool teacher might wish to use this script or the other African scripts listed above to encourage the student to investigate, write or even create their own script.

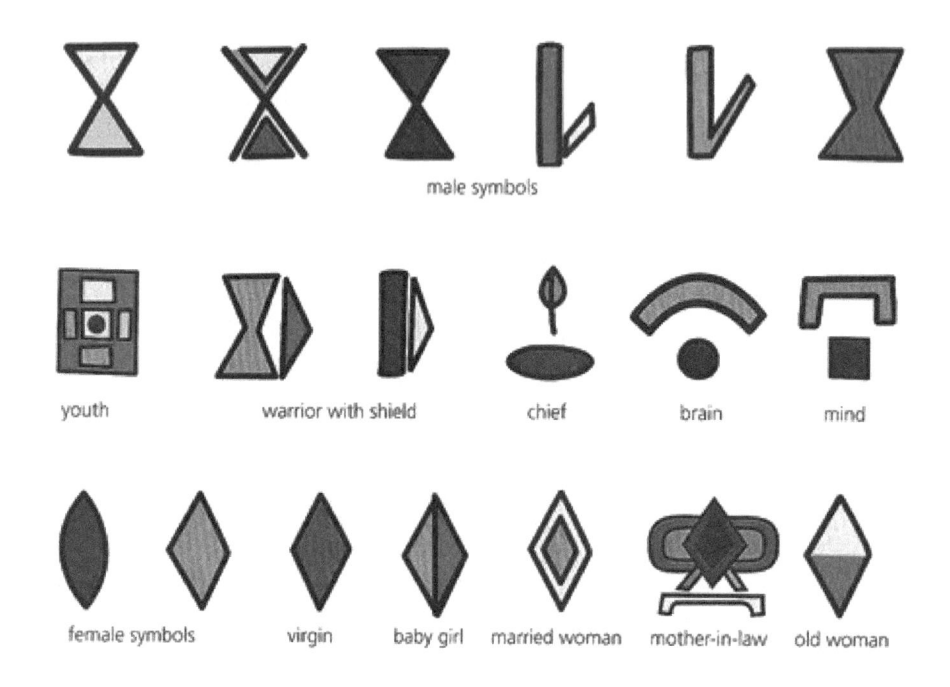

Reading and Positive Representation

Please see the books *How to Unlock Your Child's Genius* and *How to Unlock Your Family's Genius* for guidance on reading strategies.

Section 6: Mobile Learning and Online Education

Mobile Education: Apps

An "app" is short for software application. E.g., Facebook's mobile app and the term mobile education simply means the use of a variety of mobile technologies that attempt to offer a range of opportunities to improve learning through teaching, assessment and education management. This makes apps an important tool for homeschooling families.

As iPads are now outselling computers, it is no surprise to discover that 30 million apps are downloaded every day. In addition, mobile education is taking advantage of the massive growth of mobile phones, especially in emerging nations like Nigeria. For all countries, but especially in re-developing nations, Mobile Education Apps offer access to:

- ebooks
- Learning collaboration
- Learner tutor communication
- Evidence collection
- E-portfolios
- E-assessment and progress monitoring
- Task/assignment planning

Such learning strategies as those listed above are supported by apps, take for example the increasing use of apps in Africa where apps are used to disseminate health education.

Recent statistics also confirm the increased popularity of education apps, with the *Ilean II* report 2013 (an analysis of the education category of Apple's app store), which found the following:

1) Over 80% of the bestselling paid apps in the education category of the iTunes Store are targeted at children.
2) 47% (2009) top selling apps targeted young children and this number has now increased to 72%.

GSMA, an organization representing mobile operators worldwide has identified six key areas for mobile Education technology which are: vocational education and training, connected learning for children, out of classroom learning and collaboration, professional learning and development, enhanced literacy and language skills and supporting students with special needs. With such a wide application, it is not surprising that a country like the US that the sales of apps is expected to generate $38b by 2015. We are now seeing over 500,000 apps available on iTunes and an additional 300,000 plus available on Android. It is now estimated that by 2020 the sale of mobile apps will total $101 billion in the US.

However, whilst Mobile Education Apps is set to revolutionize learning, there must be caution as educators have to become increasingly aware that children and the vulnerable need to be protected from the commercialization of the digital age in the same way that children have to be protected from the harmful effects of television and film. Caution also has to be applied by educators to make sure their establishments and students have implemented device readiness, that is, they have to understand, and in some cases, liaise with app developers on the compatibility of apps to devices in places like Africa where not all mobile devices are suited to the latest high-end apps. But it cannot be denied that apps will also help the vulnerable, the marginalized and in the area of special needs education. Apps offering affordable services in speech therapy, behaviour support, sign language and communication skills, with apps like See, Touch, Learn.Pro and Pictello are just some of the popular apps.

Mobile Education Apps can achieve where politicians have failed. Apps can provide engaging education, excellence, accessibility for the underprivileged and to those homeschooled and make education inexpensive.

Online education has provided the homeschool movement with additional resources that makes learning more accessible, dynamic and engaging. This revolution started with the invention of the World Wide Web in 1969 by Tim Berners-Lee and a British engineer and computer scientist. Twenty years later in 1989 the University of Phoenix launched the first online course, which saw other universities following, before it then created the first virtual classroom. In 1997 two college students, after an amalgamation with another company, created Blackboard Inc thus creating a Learning Management System (LMS) which meant that the delivery and management of online learning could be handled efficiently as it could manage reports, keep assessments and grading. Also it could perform student messaging, display course calendars and allow for blended learning. Online learning was further developed in 1996 when another graduate, this time from Stanford University started a search engine company which eventually became known as Google. Suddenly the homeschool family had access to global education resources such as Open Yale, YouTube, BBC Bitesize, Khan Academy and Academic Earth.

Mobile Learning

The availability of mobile learning allows for "anytime and anywhere" education as students can learn on mobile devices like smart phones or ipads. Now learning was not confined to the computer, or the classroom or university campus. Online learning could enter the home of the homeschooling family and revolutionize distance learning just as the advent of the postal service; that is, as the mail correspondence course had done in the 19th and 20th centuries. This opportunity provided by new technology empowered families as it allowed the whole family, sometimes shifting the parent's role from that of teacher to facilitator.

The advantages of online learning

- People can learn anywhere and at anytime.
- Online learning allows for personalized learning.
- The learning is low cost, flexible and accessible to everyone especially those with disabilities.
- Savings are made on travel costs and time.
- Instruction is both dynamic and can use multi-media catering for a variety of learning styles.
- Group discussions allow learners, who might be dispersed, to engage with other learners and ask questions.
- Complex topics can be delivered/presented simply using text, images and animation.

The disadvantages of online learning

- Online learning does not eliminate poor technology and this can frustrate the learner.
- Online learning can prevent face-to-face learning where questions and answers can be exchanged.
- Not all students have access to multimedia and fast broadband and mobile devices.

When Identifying an online learning resource the homeschool family has to consider two methods of delivery; that is, the synchronous and asynchronous method. The virtual classroom has to have rich content, has to employ multimedia, has to have tools to allow the learner to write and engage like a chat room and have some kind of support or "scaffold". Increasingly we seem to be progressing from the instructor led to the learner-manager method of learning. Most online learning is designed with the DISC model, DISC meaning dialogue, involvement, support and control. Researchers debate as to whether the community based model is best, where the learner learns in an environment of learners and teachers. At Simon Education we have used methods from the African-Caribbean community taken from the Saturday School movement of family/community engagement with its embedded cultural literacy/Black history and bespoke learning resources. In addition, out of necessity, Simon Education has trained four types of teachers; the classroom teacher, the parent-teacher, the community teacher and the peer-teacher. From these is now emerging the virtual teacher which operates when needed.

When designing the online resources for the global African community it is not a simple matter of copying the Western design models. Eurocentric knowledge often performs the role of subjugating all other forms of knowledge, of legitimizing itself and dismissing other forms of knowledge. Online designs for the global African community must be based on a careful liberation/development assessment, one based on history and Global African studies in order to be of use. This will determine the content of the online learning.

Beside the above resources that Makeda will have to assemble she must also place cultural artifacts that are lessons in themselves. She must incorporate the African timeline, the world timeline in artifacts and thereby programme the home for success, for family learning. She must have books on Benin art, on Zulu epic poetry, artifacts on ancient maps, rap music; all, that act as guides to the voyages that Heru and Auset have taken in search of Ausar. This search is not a myth. She must have books on the many African scripts so that he can one day become a researcher despite his career and therefore be a guide, the light for others to follow. She must place djembe drums near to the maths books so that Kobi will understand the mathematics rhythms of the drum and their effect on the brain. She must have oware games by the laptop so that he learns that this game, like Ifa is a binary computer. She must the Ifa Odus, the Pert Em Heru on the table so that Kobi will know the great classic texts written by Black Africans.

Educational Design for the Virtual Classroom

The birth of the Genius educational workbooks started on the verandah of my mother's house in the eastern Caribbean accompanied by a lazy sunset that was nevertheless spectacular in its own quiet way. Although I was far from home I could still hear the anguish of children who the system said couldn't learn or branded with an almost unpronounceable condition. I had already published *How to Unlock Your Child's Genius*, which had proved to be a big success but the children wanted their book. They wanted not necessarily a book as such but to go on a learning adventure. They wanted games, riddles, proverbs, crosswords, stories and media where fantasy and learning came together. The design was simple. A workbook rigorous in the learning of English, mathematics, science and Global African Studies. Most children that have attended the various educational projects and other educational services that I have run over the last three decades do not read about themselves; do not learn about their people's achievement or think in a world view other than that of that of the West. As a result they are subjected to identity violence which results in self-hatred. This self-hated is behind all behaviour patterns in the school and home. The first thing they learn even before attending school is that there is a norm and they are not that norm, therefore their very presence is problematic in the school and beyond. My first observations when I set about creating educational services in the African-

Caribbean community was the lack of self-esteem the children displayed and that of their parents. As one parent put it at one of my parenting classes, "My child lacks confidence and doesn't perform well because I lack confidence." This realization has meant that the scaffold upon which the books were developed was the subject, Global African Studies. Put simply, the Black African child and young person has to study their history, culture, art and science, otherwise they will remain lost despite any academic success they might achieve. And despite all the qualifications they might achieve after graduating they will be a traitor to themselves, ancestors and community. They will try and figure out how to live based on the Western world view; accept propaganda as history and become loyal to the system that has mis-educated them. So their inquiry into the world and themselves must be partly informed by the systems of inquiry that their people have developed. At present it is suppressed, ignored, burnt and plundered. What remains is incomplete, so the Black African child has to emerge from institutions of learning as a researcher as opposed to a docile consumer of Western education. This means that Global African Studies has to address self-hatred whilst also promoting self-love, self-reliance, self-respect and self-determination. To achieve this, the adults of the Black African community have to ensure that their child is being educated using two curricular. The first curriculum is that which the government makes compulsory. The second curriculum is the one from their own community; an inherited but evolving curriculum. It is family centered, as opposed to the one of the government which is industry/white supremacy centered.

Global African Studies is this second and most important curriculum that allows the Black African child to inquire into the meaning of life. This curriculum is a body of knowledge that the child has to piece together again to find practical knowledge for the re-building of their communities. This curriculum has to be researched, refined, applied, reviewed and then applied again. However, reaching this body of knowledge is difficult because the Black African researcher has to rid themselves of the Western Intellectual Tradition that despises everything 'other'. It is rooted in self-indulgency of its Western world and therefore the researcher must not use its standards as the yard stick in which to inquire into indigenous African knowledge systems.

The Layout of the Workbooks and Digital Books

Each workbook covers twelve lessons, that is one lesson per week. Week 1 is English assessment week plus assignments on study skills and spelling. Week 2 is Mathematics assessment week, revision and basic science. This alternating of English and Mathematics continues throughout the book, but the workbooks are also rich with African-Caribbean proverbs, quotes of Black African heroes and empowering statements from non-African people. The assignments are aligned to a Pan-African school calendar and includes key dates such as, Black history month, Kwanzaa, Martin Luther King Day, African Remembrance, International

Women's Day, African Liberation Day and the celebration of many African heroes like Queen Nzinga and Marcus Garvey. The books, that are mapped to the Pan-African calendar that encourage the children to think critically, write, read, laugh, draw, calculate, reason, investigate and talk. But this must be in a comfortable context where they see positive and varied images of themselves and their community. At the front of the book there is a family learning profile questionnaire designed for the parents/guardians to think about their role as educators, and for the parents to complete and to encourage others to take our short online course, *How to Unlock Your Child* Genius, and our new eLearning course on *Global African Studies*. However, many children will work through these books in two formats; one being the physical books and the other being the digital book via the virtual classrooms.

The Virtual Classroom

The virtual classroom demands that you reconsider your pedagogy. At Simon Education we use the blended model where we provide online classes per term, together with home visits and small group tuition. But the virtual classroom demands and lends itself to dynamic learning, learning that can provide additional learning experiences. For this reason I have devised presentations and portals to meet the dynamic and multiple learning styles and paces that the students possess. The format that I have developed is as follows:

1) **The introductory page**
   This opening page, ideally with elements of animation to capture the imagination of the child, simply tells the child what they are going to learn and that they are about to enter into a world of learning, an adventure.

2) **The digital workbook**
   Each lesson in the workbook must be structured with short sections with increasing difficulty in each question so that the learner can grow and is not held back by a teacher who thinks that they can't manage, or don't have the skills to attempt more difficult tasks. The digital workbook has now entered the world of multi-media and therefore must hold its own so it must have bold images, imaginary images, proverbs, riddles, varied question types, headings, sub-headings, colour, variation of fonts and if possible some kind of an emotional impact. It has to be intense for the one hour is short and parents want results. The workbook must maintain the child's expectancy for they are always excited when they enter the virtual classroom and know that they can become the best in their class, or improve beyond all expectation.

3) **Worked examples**
   One of the advantages of the virtual classroom is the whiteboard that allow pages of worked examples to be used, especially in the teaching of mathematics and science. These pages become an extension of the digital workbook and give the recording of the

lesson an added life as students often watch the class recordings at their own convenience. The virtual classroom allows the pen to be given to the learner, enabling them to "come up to the board" and write answers. Here group work can easily be undertaken with breakout rooms allowing for independent work and peer support.

4) **Embedded Links**

   These embedded links can come from You Tube or any other site and are useful for making the learning experience video rich with multimedia. These links are copied in the chat section where the learner can copy them and watch them after the class. They can be film clips on literature that the learner is studying, an animation, like the film *Kirikou* that will simply inspire the leaner, or a mathematics topic like transformation of graphs that simply lend themselves to video learning. African mythology and tales are easily played using the video resources of the virtual classroom making the classroom dynamic.

   The other major use of the embedded links is that they allow for flipped learning, which is just a name given to the providing of short video clips, before the class starts, on the topic being studied so that the learner enters the class prepared and knowledgeable about topic being studied.

   At their core they promote and encourage independent learning with the learner taking responsibility to undertake these additional learning activities.

5) **Chat rooms and breakout rooms**

   The chat sections of the virtual classroom are important in allowing the learner a space to share, comment and ask a question whilst not disturbing the class too much. Indeed they become a key part of the teaching narrative that becomes less dominated by the teacher, and for the learner who is shy they perform well when they are in this virtual space, and should be discretely coaxed to being more confident in the virtual classroom.

6) **Assessing Online Learning**

   Online learning assessment can be challenging so a strict but flexible method of assessment and student progress has to be implemented. The teacher has to make almost constant notes throughout the lesson from careful observation. Sometimes this assessment will come from a simple question score, online classroom behaviour, or level of participation during the lesson, response to questions, answers submitted or/and homework submitted.

   The virtual classroom allows for quick peer assessment, strengthening the group and providing support to a student who might initially be underperforming. This information has to be collected and put in the Learning Management System where all parties: parents, students and teachers, can access it.

The teacher must allow each student the opportunity to read aloud, write on the whiteboard, answer questions individually, draw and "chat" in the chat box. They must be engaged.

Accreditation

In the homeschool movement, the digital space is where a lot of work is completed by the student and parent and it is therefore a space where digital accreditation should be encouraged as the formal accreditation system is too limited. Open digital badges are a way of acknowledging both formal and informal work and a way of supporting family learning. Digital badges are a way of registering the knowledge and skills of individuals. They are a kind of digital credential that represents an individual's skills, interests and achievements.

How Does the Digital Badge System Work?

The world of open digital badges is often referred to as an ecosystem that consists of badge issuers e.g., schools and homeschools, badge users and badge earners e.g. students. Here the issuer, that might be a homeschool collective, will set a range of competencies and assessments that the earner will have to achieve to earn the badge. The badge is hyperlinked to, say, a course or artifact where the assessment criteria are noted. The beauty of the open digital badge system is that they can be shared with other organizations that recognize the assessment criteria of the issuing organization.

Each open badge has an agreed anatomy, called the Open Badge Standard to make their currency effective and consists of:

1) Badge issuer information
2) Badge earner information
3) Course criteria (URL)
4) Evidence
5) Standards alignment
6) Taxonomy/tags.

Many homeschooling organizations should consider the open badge system as it acts as a bridge between formal and informal learning, provides excellent learner profile information and is a cost effective way of obtaining accreditation in a world where higher learning in particular is becoming increasingly expensive and therefore unaffordable for many.

Section 7: Homeschool Models

There are a number of homeschool models that families might wish to adopt depending on location, circumstances, state school support and desire for home education and community.

Here are some general models:

1) **The Family Model**
   This is when the family, normally the parents provide the bulk of the teaching and where teaching takes place within the home. The advantage of this model is that the family are able to adapt quickly to change, provide one-to-one support and have a high degree of customized learning for the child. The disadvantage of this model is that the skill set is limited to that of the parents and the child can lack socialization if not addressed by the parents.

2) **The Co-operative Model**
   This model is based on the collective or group support and is characterized by a sharing of resources and management. Central to this model is a group constitution and this model is particularly favoured by African-American and African-Caribbean families.
   The advantage of this model is that it has a greater pool of skills and knowledge than a single family and perhaps greater financial resource base. If one of the parents is absent for any reason then this does not have such a major impact on the homeschool as compared to the single family model. The disadvantage of this model is that decision making can be slow, group disagreements can undermine the performance of the homeschool collective with members leaving and therefore undermining the morale of the group.

3) **The Hybrid Model**
   This follows the single family model but here families can 'shop' in the larger state education system for educational resources in order for their child to attend individual classes. This relies heavily on state education becoming more accommodating towards homeschool families.

Whilst these models are some to be considered the homeschool family also needs to be clear on its educational philosophy. Below are some methods approaches.

The Simon Method
This method is based on the books by the educationalist and author, David Simon. He has championed education innovation within the African-Caribbean community in London and the Black Diaspora. His method of education centers around the family and the community taking on various roles as teachers, learning coaches and the manufacturers of educational resources. Central to this philosophy is self and community development.
The Charlotte Mason Method
This method is founded on the belief that children learn best from real life experiences and the belief that the 'whole' child should be educated, therefore there should be creative time and play allocated to the learning experience.
The Socratic Method
This method is centered around the development stages of the child's cognitive development in terms of their analytical, concrete, and abstract thinking.
Eclectic Method
A mix of different approaches to homeschooling.
Unit Studies Method
This method focuses on specific interest that the child is attracted to and this method therefore hopes that this interest will act as a kind of catalyst and gain the study skills that will allow them to access other areas.
Unschooling Method
A method that does not use a specific curriculum or formal lesson plans and is very much in the tradition of John Holt.

These approaches have been adopted by Western families (with the exception of the Simon method) following their traditional homeschool paths, having been inspired by the two roots of Western homeschooling, John Holt and Raymond Moore. It was John Holt, author of Teach Your Own (1981) who said that "schools are incompetent at their work, even as they define it, having found it easier to blame all their failures on their students (p 9). This statement perhaps indicates the frustration and anger that homeschool families have towards the State education system. Importantly he goes on to identify the civil liberties of the child and the systematic infringements that the school engages in. These infringements include:

1) Keeping permanent records of children's school performance.
2) Keeping school records secret from children and/or their parents.
3) Making those records accessible to others without the permission of the children or their parents.
4) Filling records with malicious and derogatory remarks.
5) Compulsory psychological testing of children.
6) Labeling children as having an imaginary and incurable learning difficulty/disability.

However, in black African communities, these approaches and personalities have not necessarily been the engine behind their homeschooling. And we must remember that in America at least, African-American families have sought to homeschool their children for different reasons. Research by Tal Levy indicates that the more integrated the school system is the more likely that the legislators would adopt homeschooling legislation. He points out that between 1990 and 2000 homeschooling has increased by 500%, indicating that desegregation in America (1954 Brown v. Board of Education) partly fuelled the white middle class homeschool movement. To discover the roots of the global Black homeschool movement we have to look deep into history, into Global African Studies and the quest for knowledge. Throughout Africa people adhered to the philosophy of Ubuntu which could mean anything from vital force to oneness, and it is this attempt by African people all over the world to once again be engaged in attaining Ubuntu (Bantu), that is oneness with God that sees families not only seeking to educate their children for work, but educate their children to achieve this oneness, Ubuntu.

Makeda's Story: The Great Curriculum of Ausar

Makeda was now tired and so when she opened the book looking for more answers it should have provided her with some peace but instead the pages were themselves almost screaming. There on the beach, holding a great sword made by one of the thousands of Kushite blacksmith was Heru, shouting to the world.

"I can see again! I will find Ausar! I will piece it back together again!" The Goddess of the Ethiopean Ocean rose up bellowing at Heru, find Ausar, find your father! With her hand she slapped the sands by the feet of Heru until, suddenly as more dark clouds came, all about Heru was a map of ancient and modern cities, castles and palaces; underground schools and hidden scrolls. It was, she would later be told, the Map of the *Seven Teachers*. Each teacher was located in a different place, a different time zone and each held a piece of the Great Curriculum of Ausar. As Makeda was trying to make sense of the story, Sankofa flew down and landed by Heru who immediately grasped the giant birds feathers, swung up onto the back of the bird and with his sword still held high the bird took off into the night sky as rain threatened. Sankofa knew exactly where to travel. And as the bird flew Heru saw strange things. He saw an Africa in deep trouble. He saw an African with great migrations travelling across the continent as one invasion after the other tore this great land part. Teachers, scribes, professors of Jenne, Timbuktu and Sankore were being hunted down,

murdered. Magnificent libraries of Africa were being burnt to the ground, their conquerors shouting:

"You are a people of nothing. You will never know your history again!" Whilst most teachers were murdered with a brutality that the history books of the conquerors would leave out, one or two escaped. They went deep into the forests and there, away from the murderous invaders, built communities, societies that barely eked out a living but were safe for the time being. As the years went by, these same teachers, in secret, taught those they trusted, about the *Great Curriculum of Ausar*, even though they only had their own little scroll. They taught what they could, around night fires, or deep in the bush, in the hope that one day Great Africa would rise again. What was of utmost importance was secrecy, so they ingeniously devised secret languages, secret scripts of their now underground academies and universities. His first stop was to the first teacher Auset. Since the invasion of Africa, she lived deep into the forests. She, was now fighting against the superstition of people around her. The great institutions that her predecessors had founded were destroyed, and the science and technology were understood by fewer and fewer people as there were no longer the schools, colleges and universities to pass on and develop this information. Generations of black Africans to come would not know of great teachers like Auset. She, this increasingly lonely master knew this, but there was a challenge. The only way that the great teachings could be passed on to the next generation was through art, storytelling, secret lessons. When Heru stood before her she was at first puzzled as to why he had come. Who was he, she thought to herself, but then she recognized the bird, Sankofa. He sat at her feet which was blessed with cowry shells wrapped around her ankle.

"Why have you come?" Her voice was soft, but yet secretive for she now not only lived deep in the bush but was a commander of spirits, those spirits that gathered as armies waiting and seeing the start of the Arab slave trade, a brutal war on Black Africa that would see millions butchered, dismembered and killed. She also saw, some eight hundred years in the distance, European slave ships sailing quietly to Africa. Despite these horrific sights she stood at her post devotedly, training her spirits to defend their people by helping them to remember and keep their culture.

"I've come for the scroll, for the *Great Curriculum of Ausar*." Auset mused, looking beyond the young man, looking behind him to see which ancestors had accompanied him, though he knew little of their presence.

"The scroll can only be read by those who have cultivated the *Melanin Eye*, and this eye opens, when the other two close. It is not for me to give this scroll to you, but your spirit to read it as you sleep." Though Heru was confused he obeyed her words and continued through time and terrain of the African forest in search of all the teachers of the *Great Curriculum of*

Ausar. Each one that he came to was living in hiding for many were still being hunted down by future colonialists and missionaries of Africa, who would find them, burn their books, as they forced Africans to convert to their religions that saw their God. In truth, it wasn't about religion, it was about gold, land and slaves. Each time Heru came to one of these teachers they told him about arithmetic and numerical sequences, formulas of God, or rhetoric to argue that there was only one God, or told him about the science of astrology and celestial paths, and powerful planets and their covert relationship with the earth. He listened to them and learnt their proverbs, poems, riddles and prayers. He learnt about their binary computers, that bemused anthropologists would later call oracles, and their mathematics and thinking designs to understand apparent chaos, to understand patterns in nature, to understand the incidence of fractals and the algorithm and science of each Ifa odu in order to unlock reality. Yet these teachers were training armies that would soon be required to fight, and fight like hell as invaders would come. The story that Makeda read ended with Heru returning to the Land of Kush, and there on the beach with his mother looking on and the *Great Curriculum of Ausar* unified in his heart, he stood there beside Sankofa with his sword raised high and shouted to the world. "*I am Heru, and I have the Great Curriculum of Ausar*. Africans of the future, live by your great traditions or die."

Makeda closed the book suddenly. She ran to the window to look for the great bird but it wasn't there. Perhaps it had never been there. All she knew as she heard Kobi playing downstairs was that she had to be the seven teachers, that the *Great Curriculum of Ausar* was the only way she could educate her child or any other child for that matter. Suddenly the seven classrooms and the seven teachers were staring her in the face.

Section 8: Trends in Employment

Training the parent-teacher

As part of your preparing to become a homeschooler, the parent - depending on education and expertise, should undertake some formal training in the teaching of English, Mathematics and Science. The training should cover topics such as knowing the national curriculum even though the parents might wish not to strictly follow this curriculum; teaching methods, assessment methods, behaviour management, resources, family learning and monitoring of progress.

Whilst these subjects are important the parent-teacher who is homeschooling their child will need a range of skills that might also include art and design and physical education. Of course the parent-teacher is not expected to teach all subjects but competency in some is very useful. A dual curriculum should be at work at all times, that is national curriculum of the country where the family reside and a second curriculum that stems from the community that the family are from. This curriculum is essentially about power. It should be designed to empower the family and community, therefore it is multi-faceted. A single parent-teacher cannot administer this curriculum alone. It needs a team of teachers: classroom teacher, parent-teacher, community teacher, peer teacher and virtual teacher. And what will this second curriculum consists of? All the subjects necessary for the family and community to fulfill themselves and become self-empowered, self-sufficient and self-determining.

This in-house teacher training should be continuous and planned so that as the child develops and progresses in their academic and social abilities the parent-teacher is able to keep up and maintain their competency.

This training should be both formal and informal. I have found that listening to debates on education and reading other authors to be of vital importance including attending conferences on education.

The Homeschool and New Employment Trends

The task of homeschooling your child will inevitably mean that the parent or parents will have to sacrifice part or all of their income to undertake the teaching of their child/children. This will result in loss of earnings, perhaps create financial instability in the security of the family and can indeed undermine the whole project of homeschooling. However, when one becomes aware of the change and opportunities in employment trends then the family can plan income streams which might even increase the long term financial stability of the home. The family will now be in a position to keep developing their employment portfolio, providing them not only multiple streams of income but also a mindset focused on self-determination.

So what are these new employment trends that will support the homeschool?

1. An online business selling a product or service
2. An eBay business.

3. An online eBook business.
4. Selling of homemade craft goods e.g., herbal creams, carvings etc
5. Selling marketing services using social media platforms.
6. Selling at a local market.
7. Affiliate marketing.
8. Earning from a home based franchise.
9. Tutoring other children with skills you the parent-teacher now has.

In his book, *Work it Out,* Des McCabe recommends that someone wishing to enter into the new world of work should change their mindset and look at themselves in six new ways and ask themselves these six questions.

1. What skills do I possess that could help to create products or services I could offer?
2. What experience (both formal and informal) do I have that could be useful in creating new products or services?
3. What qualifications (even informal qualifications) do I have that could be useful in creating new products or services?
4. How might things that I like to do be turned into new products or services? Especially things that might just be seen as hobbies.
5. How can the areas that I am really interested in be turned into new products and services? That is, what are my passions in life and how can I earn from them.
6. How can my real ambitions for the future give me new and exciting ideas for new products and services? To achieve this you need an adventurous mind!

These employment initiatives and the dynamism associated with them creates an entrepreneurial spirit that is central to a creative homeschool where the family is constantly growing and developing as it accumulates new skills and opportunities. It will lead to the child/children becoming apprentices in a range of employment areas and further develop and strengthen family learning as the income streams grow.

It is advisable that Makeda undertakes a course like Global African Studies: an eLearning Course for she will study models of success. She will study how Africans constantly developed trade routes from the interior of Africa to the coast and then to India, China, the Americas, and how they manufactured and sold, and bartered and exchanged. She will study people like Madam C. J. Walker and her multilevel marketing systems; she will study Marcus Garvey and his investment bonds to launch his shipping company; she will study Black Wall Street and how they created their own bank to finance black businesses; she will study the Windrush Generation of Caribbean people who came over to England in the late 1940s to help rebuild post-war Britain and she will learn how, unable to get mortgages to purchase properties to live, how they used an old West African savings scheme known as Susu (or pardner in Jamaica) to raise finance to purchase their first homes. This is the curriculum and education that will ultimately secure her child's future.

Section 9: Recommended Books

The 10 most important books on educating your child

Rank	Title
1.	*How to Unlock Your Child's Genius* by David Simon
2.	*Smart Moves* by Carla Hannaford
3.	*Why Children Can't Read* by Diane McGuinness
4.	*How to Unlock Your Family's Genius* by David Simon
5.	*How Children Fail* by John Holt
6.	*Black Children: Their Roots, Culture and Learning Styles* by Janice E. Hale
7.	*Reading Reflex* by Carmen and Geoffrey McGuinness
8.	*Harvesting New Generations* by Useni Eugene Perkins
9.	*The Miseducation of the Negro* by Carter G. Woodson
10.	*The Learning Revolution* by Vos Dryden and Jeanette Gordon

Section 10: Health and Learning

Move-2-Genius is a series of movements, postures and games to improve a person or child's breathing, flexibility, alignment, relaxation (stress relief) and thinking skills. *Move-2-Genius* works and develops the 205 bones of the body and 506 muscles of the body. It develops fine motor skills and gross motor skills, through movement, rhythm games and thinking exercises. It has been designed to work the motor centres of the brain that are located near the cortex. Whilst some of the learning designed and presented in this book is sedentary, *Move-2-Genius* incorporates movement as a key tool for learning. The brain consists of 100 billion brain cells called neurons. The brain, through activity, creates networks with these cells which 'fire'. This brain activity/firing must also be supported with correct nutrition including multi-vitamins and minerals, iron and B complex, Omega 3, 6 and 9, plus sleep, water and meditation. *Move-2-Genius* exercises, based on ancient African and Ancient Indian yoga, acknowledges that learning must not be sedentary.

Move-2-Genius introduction:

Introduction to the skeletal system, muscular system, the respiratory system and the nervous system. Awareness of the everyday abuse of our bodies and minds is one of the starting points of this series of movement exercises.

The Skeletal System

The skeletal system consists of bones that form a moveable framework for the body and to give protection to the internal parts of the body like the brain (skull) and lungs (rib cage). The skeleton consists of 206 bones, almost half of which are in the feet and hands. Move-2-Genius is designed to work all these muscles and to raise awareness of their care.

A muscle is a fibrous organ that contracts and produces motion through its connection with bones, cartilage, ligaments, fasciae and skin. The muscular system consists of more than 650 individual muscles which take up approximately 40% of our body weight. The muscles of the skeleton work in groups in opposition to each other, e.g., the biceps and triceps.

The Brain

The brain, which weighs 2% of our body weight, can be said to be the headquarters of the central nervous system and its 10 billion cells transmit messages to and from all parts of the body. Such activity means that it requires 20% of the energy that the body produces. The human brain starts to develop as soon as the sperm penetrates the egg. Here the zygote begins to divide until there are hundreds of cells and by the fourteenth day a small section of multiplying cells begin to fold in on itself. This cell division continues and by the eighth week the brain has developed its three parts. The three parts of the brain are: the reptilian brain, which was the first part of the brain to develop, the mammalian brain which was the second part to develop and the cortex or higher brain which is responsible for higher order thinking and makes up 80% of the human brain.

Neurologists are now finding that the area of the brain that coordinates physical movement, the cerebellum, also coordinates thoughts; therefore, movement aids learning and brain development. The word emotion means to move. The process of learning to undertake a physical act, like Move-2-Genius is at first taken up by neurons in the cortex where new learning occurs, however, once this activity becomes automatic the brain function moves to the lower parts of the brain, thereby freeing up areas in the brain for new learning to take place in the cortex.

However, when talking about the brain and the learning process we have to also talk about melanin. Melanin is a complex molecule and found in practically all living organisms to various degrees. In T. Owen Moore's book, ***The Science of Melanin: Dispelling the Myths*** (1995) he outlines the many benefits attributed to melanin. He writes:

1) Melinated skin provides protection against the harmful effects of ultraviolet radiation.
2) Melanin can protect cells and tissues against oxidizing conditions.
3) The bioelectronic properties of melanin facilitate nerve conduction and these regions of the brain with high melanin concentration generate greater activity than non-melinated brain regions.

In essence Dr. Owens is stating that the bioelectronic properties of melanin facilitate nerve conduction, and as it is found in the nervous system, it heightens mental awareness, speeds reaction time and helps to enable the brain to transmit neural impulses. He goes on to state:

> In other words, melanin is involved in the transformation
>
> of one form of energy into another by coupling together
>
> two different physical states (vibrations and electricity). (p.34)

We can see from the above information that any movement and learning system has to understand the workings of melanin and therefore devise learning systems and promote learning activities, styles and paces that recognize all the wonderful properties of melanin.

Move-2-Genius is a series movement exercises that has been designed working with melinated children and observing them learning. That is, observing them totally engaged, totally bored; observing them rocking to some unknown rhythm in their heads, 'bouncing' into the class, learning intuitively, winning disproportionate races during school sports day whilst on occasions hating their school yet wanting desperately to learn, but not learn what school has to offer them. *Move-2-Genius* has been developed having counseled thousands of parents on how to engage their child in their learning. I have observed how they have sat down, gotten up from a seated position; how they have shaken my hand, walked across the playground. I have observed the texture of their skins, their hair; their use of skin lighteners, the locking of their hair, their talk, their accents and their myriad of health issues. Of course, I make no claims about these movements and games and would always advise anyone to go and seek advice from a qualified health practitioner, but I simply outline the Move-2-Genius exercises that have given so many children, young people, parents and teachers, fun, self-awareness and discipline.

Stage 1: Creating the African Learning Tree

The teaching narrative is centered around the introduction of the systems of learning that Africans have developed, based on the knowledge that the human spiritual anatomy has faculties which need to be awakened. Many of the so-called learning difficulties within the education system can be corrected by allowing students the opportunity to move, breathe and relax so that they are not learning in a tense environment. Similarly, this is the case with teachers whose health often deteriorates once they become teachers.

First series of postures: Stretching and breathing, learning to the final posture of the Learning Tree.

Stage 2: Sankofa

This series of postures (asanas) starts with the Sun salute. An acknowledgement of the Sun and its role in the formation of melanin, its process of photosynthesis and its impact on the pineal gland. Move-2-Genius is based on science which includes neuroscience. Once the Learning Tree posture has been achieved the mind will have become quiet. The focus of the postures is on the spine and breathing from the lower sections of the lungs to ensure maximum oxygenation of the blood. This purification of the blood and the removal of stale air from the lungs should improve clarity of thinking, help to clean the blood although blood cleansers should also be used under the guidance of a qualified practitioner. The mind is now quiet. The "tree" is established.

Stage 3: Finding Peace

This series of postures that mostly take place on the floor are designed to manipulate spine and all the muscles of the body, leading to the final posture which is that of absolute relaxation, or known in African yoga as the mummy pose. Starting from the cat pose, to familiar yoga poses such as the twist, fish pose, head-stand and plough, finally leading to the mummy/corpse pose. The benefits of the pose are many; improve peristalsis action, improved posture, improved bowel movement, improved blood and lymph circulation; all resulting in the cleansing of the body.

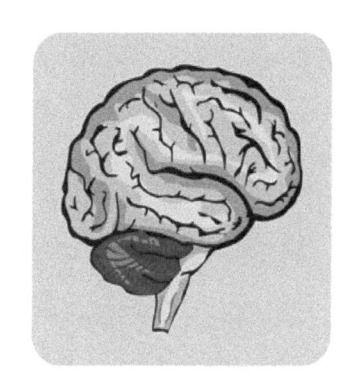

Move-2-Genius: Breathing

Breathing and Respiratory System

When you breathe (normally 16 to 18 times per minute) you only expel approximately two-thirds of the air from your lungs, whilst the other one third of the air remains in your lungs. Deep breathing exercises in Move-2-Genius and simply being aware of your breathing allows your whole respiratory system (rib cage and diaphragm etc) to work more efficiently. This results in greater oxygenation of the blood and improved cell activity.

Move-2-Genius Games: Think Before You Move

This game is designed to support children's thinking and develop their memory skills.

How the game is played

1. Four children stand in an arc.
2. Each player is assigned a number, e.g Player 1, Player 2 (who holds the ball behind their back), Player 3, Player 4
3. Two other children stand face-to-face, approximately 1 metre apart. The player with his/her back to the other 4 players is known as **the Thinker**, whilst the other child they are facing is known as **the Strategist**.
4. The Strategist has five 'moves' whereby they instruct the players to move the ball to their left or right, or move the ball two places to the left of right. Typically the Strategist will say, whoever has the ball pass it one place to the right/left, or Player 1 swap with Player 4.
5. The red ball always starts with Player 2.
6. The Strategist also has two swaps which count as a 'move' where they can tell Player 1 to swap places with Player 4.
7. Once five 'moves' have been made by The Strategist, he/she then asks The Thinker to turn around and face the Players and points to the Player that has the ball behind their back. If he/she points to the right Player then they have won the game, if not then they have lost the game.

The object of the game is to have the Thinker decide where the ball has been moved to after the strategist has given 5 orders to the players to have the ball moved. The game increases in difficulty as more balls are added, totaling three, – red, gold and green.

The game helps support a child's thinking skills, strategizing, listening skills and teamwork.

This game has another key use for children learning coding as it helps them to understand simple algorithms.

Brain Food

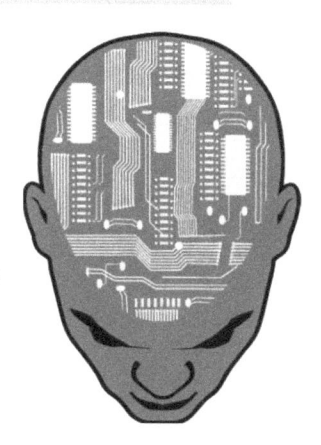

Now that we have looked at the intelligence system of the body that is not entirely based in the brain we now have to consider natural foods of the body. Glucose is an important nutrient for the brain and nervous system. Humans use plants to gather the Sun's energy and when we eat these plants energy is released from the carbohydrate in the form of glucose which is used by the brain and the cells of the body. Another important nutrient is the essential fats: omega-3 (polyunsaturated) fat e.g., EPA and DHA, omega-6 (polyunsaturated) fat e.g., GLA and AA. Both omega-3 and omega-6 are essential for good brain function.

Brain Foods are:

Omega-3	Omega-6	Omega-9
Flax (linseed)	Safflower	
Hemp	Sunflower	
Pumpkin	Sesame	
Walnut	Hemp	
	Pumpkin	

There are three types of phospholipids: Phosphatidyl choline, phosphatidyl serine and phophatidyl dimethylethanolamine (DMAE). Phospholipids are considered to the 'intelligent' fats in the brain as they help the substance called myelin that assists in efficient brain signals and therefore help in aiding good memory as they help make acetylcholine, the brain's memory neurotransmitter. The reader might consider supplementing their diet with a food rich in these phospholipids, such as lecithin.

Amino Acids

Amino Acids are the building blocks from which proteins are formed and the end products of protein digestion. There are twenty-two known amino acids which must all be present in the diet for the body to work properly. Eight of these amino acids are called essential amino acids and cannot, like to others, be manufactured by the body. They therefore must be obtained from our food or from supplements.

The 22 Amino Acids

Alanine	*Leucine
Arginine	*Lysine
Asparagine	*Methionine
Aspartic acid	Ornithine
Cysteine	*Phenylalanine
Cystine	Proline
Glutamic acid	Serine
Glutamine	*Threonine

Glycine	*Trytophan
*Histidine	Tyrosine
*Isoleucine	*Valine

*Essential amino acids

A ninth amino acid called histidine, is also considered an essential amino acid as it is essential for infants and children. When taking amino acids the major vitamins should also be taken that are involved in their metabolism.

Whilst ensuring that the family has the correct nutrients is vital so is the maintaining of the body through correct rest, sleep and cleansing of the body sometimes known as detoxing.

1) Take omega-3 and omega-6 rich foods or supplements.
2) Take extra antioxidant nutrients vitamins A, C and E, selenium and zinc.
3) Eat high fiber and fresh vegetables and fruit containing antioxidant nutrients that limit the harmful effects of free radicals that cause cell damage.
4) Try not to expose your family to toxins from heavy metals, petrochemicals and pesticides.
5) Take a recommended amount of water each day, sometimes with lemon or cider vinegar to maintain the correct alkaline balance.
6) If you are taking antibiotics discuss with your doctor how you can repair your bowel flora.
7) Take regular exercise and undertake deep breathing exercise to remove stale air from the lower regions of the lungs and to oxygenate the blood correctly.
8) Avoid being angry, tired and depressed.
9) Rest, sleep and meditate.
10) Eliminate or reduce your intake of refined foods and foods that are high in yeast, sugar and salt. This applies to dairy products.
11) Help your liver, kidneys, intestines and bowels by giving them rest, water and cleansing herbs like milk thistle seed and chicory root.

Section 11: Who Will Name Our Children

For African parents who keep their child in the Eurocentric education system or one based on the nineteenth century European industrial model then their child will leave school or graduate without having attended the most important of all lessons and or lectures, lessons that will have to be delivered by the community. What are these lessons? The first is on Global African Studies which empowers the individual in addressing the immediate and future challenges that their community will face. These modules/lessons mostly mostly be delivered by a team of teachers from the African community themselves. The parent-teacher, the community-teacher, the peer-teacher have to deliver this curriculum but first they have to know it themselves. The curriculum is the African Tree of Knowledge, and its seven components. So what must be taught, when, where and by whom. Below is a summary outline of the Global African Studies and teaching methods that might be considered:

Stage 1: Auset /Sankofa Stage

topic	**The formation of the universe and humankind** - How to research - African mythology and cosmology - The movement of the tectonic plates - From Pangaea to Africa - The first humans and the Rift Valley
Key components of the lesson plan	

Stage 2: Sebek Stage

	Classical African Civilisation - Nubia, Egypt, Ethiopia and Black India - Hieroglyphs and Rock Art - Yoga and African Spiritual Science
Key lesson	- The Metu Neter and the Human Brain - The Shabaka Stone/African Philosophy - The practice and philosophy of African Yoga
Class activities	Students should have the opportunity to write the Metu Neter script and undertake basic African/Black Indian yoga postures.

Stage 3

	Africa of the Middle Ages: Art and Literature - Maps and documents of Africa - African art

African-Caribbean Naming Ceremony: Who Will Name Our Children?

The naming of the child is a critical stage in their and the families' education, for it is a community act. It is the naming ceremony that Makeda wanted but didn't know quite where to go to get this service and it is the ceremony the mother of Heru in the book that she read must have gone, for Heru knew his spiritual quest in life was to find Ausar, the great God within. Below is a schedule for the naming of the child and some commentary notes to explain its significance.

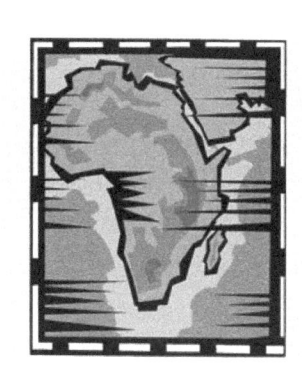

Naming Ceremony Schedule

Activity	Notes
Pre-initiation / Pre-Naming Ceremony	
Choosing of the day	• Day chosen should preferably be a full moon to generate a positive force
The Naming Ceremony space - purification	• Cleaning of the space with water and ammonia • Burning of incense (frankincense and myrrh)
The ambiance - Joyful music should be played	• As this is the child's first initiation joy must be present to formally welcome the child into the community
Welcome and introduction - Call names of elders - Call names of grandparents - Call names of distinguished members - Call names of parents	• Seat key family members on top table • People stand when name is called
Explanation of the naming ceremony and its significance - Name to remind child of their spiritual mission in life - Name contains words/phonemes of power/vibrations that speak to the	• Quote from African texts • Look at some African names and explain meaning

child's soul	
Pouring of libation - to honour, respect and remember the Ancestors - to 'feed' the ancestors	• Accompanied by drumming • Response from audience- Ashe/Amen
Ancestor shrine - its function and purpose - the role of ancestors in African communities - the Ancestors as community guides	• the role and function of the shrine • Food shared amongst those that attend at the end
Libation prayer/poem - calling of names - Wetting the Ground	• Drumming • Men pour rum, women pour water second
Cutting of Kola nuts - for wise counsel - contents of the Kola nuts	• the sharing of the Kola nuts • the significance of the Kola nut • caffeine and wise counsel
Invoking guidance from Elegba, Sebek - we ask that they give counsel, be it insight, dreams or intuition	• our ideas about ourselves as divine beings must be in harmony with divine law
Reflection & Pledge - all family members and adults present must visualize the child being brought up correctly, living in harmony with divine law	• Audience encouraged to visualize this child being brought up correctly • Family members pledge to help guide the child
Blessing of the gathering - their role in the child's upbringing - challenges the child will face	• gathering are not only guests • who will step forward and help support the child
Announcing of the name - tradition and culture	• name first whispered to the child • the arrival of the child
Blessing of the child - blessing from the seven psychic centers of the spirit - placing water and rum on child to signify	• Poem/drumming
Meaning of the name - explanation from parents	• Parents explain the meaning of the name
Reading of African proverbs - counseling from our culture	• Group discussion on chosen proverbs • Parents read the proverbs
Gifts of the family - presentation of gifts to the family - the need for the community to support and share	• presentation of the gifts to the family • Gifts of song, poetry or rap
Guidance to the family	• audience asked to state how they will

- their role to guide the spiritual development of the child - their role to gain insight into the child's spiritual journey - their role to educate the child	help support and guide the child and family

Resources

1. Books and proverbs
2. Shrine items
3. Plants - water and rum (unopened)

Layout

1. top table
2. shrine (table covered in white cloth)
3. rostrum
4. table and chairs for the audience

Preparing of the Naming Ceremony Space

Choosing the day

The day of the naming ceremony is normally chosen by the paternal grandparents. The day of the naming ceremony is normally 4 to 8 days after the birth of the child.

Commentary

Those who will name our children will be those who have dedicated themselves to learn traditional and modern African science related to the birth and naming of a child. They will know the foods that the mother and father needed to have taken before the child was conceived; they will know the yoga postures that will assist in the delivery, breathing locks to control the bodies' energy systems; they will know about the key nutrients so that the mother and baby are not depleted of essential nutrients to aid recovery and growth. Those who will name our children will know the science of DNA and its codes and the binary computer systems of Africa and the African Diaspora and the verses with their accompanying algorithms that were designed to unlock the child's genius. Those who will name the African child will have studied the cosmos; know that they were part of the Big Bang, for African cosmology has said so; said that beyond the 14 million years before the formation of the universe small was big, and there was no beginning, and they will hear the sound of cosmic back ground radiation which is really a song, a universal melody full of mathematical improvisations that the creators of the binary computer systems studied when they created Ifa. Yes, it is they who will teach the melanin child, all children, how to stand before the great Sun, understand the science of its radiation and how it impacts on the child's pineal gland and tell this melanin child, you are blessed, we are blessed.

Purification

The naming ceremony space should be cleaned both physically and spiritually.

The physical cleanse should be with water and ammonia and the spiritual cleanse should be with the burning of incense. This cleansing removes negative energies from the naming ceremony space.

Commentary

Who will cleanse the naming ceremony space for the child to be named will be those who have purified themselves. The legacy of oppression inflicted upon the Black African, whether they are in Africa or the Diaspora, has left the African traumatized in some way, whether they realize it or not. The physical scars may well be gone by the time the child's eyes open, but they will be greeted by a community whose behaviour is still orchestrated by these physical and psychological horrors. The child will at first see the beautiful world through its innocent brown eyes but as it grows, the many guns of society will force it to look at the world with inferiority. These agencies will tell the child to put his or her hands in the air and look at their world; to hate the world of their heritage. So a masquerade will appear. Fantasies of the adults parading themselves with wigs, bright clothes, and ridiculous smiles, and books with big bold words of western writers, and paintings of European artists, and operas of western composers. They will see many of their adults trying to be something they are not; crying behind the masks. These adults can't name the child, for they can't even call their own names. Those who will name the child and purify the space will be those who can remember how to sit like they did in Black India, in that lotus position. It will be those who can remember how to meditate and watch the tyranny of thought until it becomes quiet to allow a greater intelligence to emerge. It will be those who will study the poetry and mathematics of the world to listen to the muses of the oracles of Africa. These are the people who will purify the space, not only for the child to be named but for him or her to grow, learn, develop and blossom into a beautiful human being.

Purification of those Administering the Naming Ceremony Ritual

Those who administer the naming ceremony should also undergo purification by:

1) Removing all negative thoughts from their minds.
2) Cleansing before the naming ceremony.
3) Abstaining from drinking alcohol and eating heavily salted food.

They should also focus on the naming ceremony and gain insight into the child's incarnation objective. The attire of those administering the ceremony should be white clothing, quartz for spiritual protection and the aunghk, an African symbol of democratic power.

Preparation of the Family and Child

The parents should spend the day before the ceremony reflecting on the child's name and how they will help the child to fulfill his/her name's purpose.

The day before the naming ceremony and leading up to it parents should eat unsalted food for clarity of mind.

On the day of the ceremony the parents should bathe and wear white and dress the baby in white linen.

Welcome and Introduction

The narrative for the welcoming to be spoken by the African priest.

- Greetings to the Elders, brothers and sisters and children present.
- We welcome the two families who have come together to put on this naming ceremony.
- Welcome to the naming ceremony of …………………………….
- My name is ………………………… and I will conduct this naming ceremony in accordance with traditional African protocols.

  Continuing protocol:
- Ask two families to stand before the community; mention the importance of their role.
- So in accordance with African tradition all ceremonies must open with libation.

- First, an explanation as to what is libation. Libation is the honouring, the respecting and the remembering of our Ancestors. And it is also an invitation to the Ancestors to be present in the ceremony for they help to guide the community.
- When pouring libation we ask those who want to pour libation to step forward and do so.
- (optional) Men pour the rum and women pour the water into the plant that represents the earth.
- Explain the importance of the naming ceremony

What is the Meaning of the Naming Ceremony

The naming ceremony has different names in traditional African society. In the Kamitic tradition of Ancient Egypt it was known as the Nekhab, in the Yoruba tradition of Nigeria it is known as Din To by the Akan tradition.

The naming ceremony that usually takes place between the 4th to 8th day after the birth, fulfils two functions:

1) It is a ceremonial contract that sees the parents pledge to the child, community and the Ancestors that they will help to cultivate the child and see that it lives by the values of its name.
2) It is a time when the family announces the existence of a new member of the community.

Why is the Name Important

The pronunciation of the name carries sound; sound is vibration and this vibration directed at a child repeatedly has the effect on the spirit of the child.

As the name has meaning it is therefore the child's tool of self-development, a tool to remind the child of their divine destiny in the world.

Libation

Stage 1

Cutting of the Kolanuts (called Oji in Igbo)

The Kolanut ritual has three steps:

1) The presentation of the Kolanuts.

2) Breaking of kolanuts.
3) Distribution of kolanuts.

Kolanuts are cut and shared at all important gatherings. These seeds contain caffeine which makes the consumer alert and therefore fit for wise counsel. A prayer is said as the Kola nut is being cut.

Song of the Kolanut

Oji, Kolanut seed of Chuku

Give wise counsel

So this child may sing

Melodies of Oshun

And know divine harmony

Oji, Kolanut seed of Neter

Hear the prayer of Child-spirit

So they may dance with Auset

And know her hymns of devotion to God.

Oji, Kolanut seed of Obatala

Counsel and guide this child

So they might beat spiritual drums

To summon the joy of Yemaya

Oji, blessed Kolanut seed of God

Sing, dance and let Ancestors know

That we are this child's guide.

- Protocol to be followed once poem is recited
- The Kola nut once cut will be shared amongst all adults.

Stage 2

The Pouring of Libation

This ceremony is known in the Eastern Carriacou as 'Wetting the Ground'.

Narrative to be spoke by the African Priest

As we are going to pour libation then we would like you all to assist and by responding to the end of each verse recited with the word *ashe*, which is simply the African word for Amen, which in itself is an African name of an aspect of God.

We invite all those who wish to participate in the pouring of libation to come up and pour either the water or rum into the plant which represents the earth.

The protocol is as follows:

1) Women pour water (using their right hand) onto the plant first, remembering their Ancestors.
2) Men pour rum (using their left hand) into the plant second, remembering their Ancestors.
3) At all times all adults present pledge to live by the high standards of their Ancestors and to support/guide the child.

Commentary

Who will pour libation and call the names of the great African heroes, the majority of who have been left out of modern school history books. Those who do will have to know the names of all the great Africans, know the Great African woman and her blessed mitochondrial DNA whose wonders scientists now study; know the Africans who built ancient Kush, ancient Kamit (Egypt), ancient Ethiopia, ancient Ile Ife; to Ghana, Mali and Songhai; the names of those that carried the big stones that built ancient Zimbabwe. Who will call the names of the artist whose hands chiseled and crafted the great sculptures of Benin and Ife. Who will stand proud and shout out the names of those Africans who fought against the slave wars launched by the Arabs, the Europeans. These kings and queens that had to become generals and send armies of men and women to defend their land, their gold, their women. Who will call the names of Yaa Asantewa, Nzingha, Paul Bogle, Gabriel Prosser, Nat Turner, Harriett Tubman, Marcus Garvey, Amy

Garvey, Malcolm X, Martin Luther King and those that lie in the unmarked and mass graves of Namibia? Who will rediscover the unmarked battlefields where brave men and women fought defending Africa, defending their land, culture and their children?

So when libation is poured the community should recognize that sacrifice of those who have gone before and the wise counsel that they can give to the present community. This is the child's tradition. After libation is poured the priest/community teacher should offer advice to the two families.

Invoking of Elegba/Sebek for Guidance: Our Mental Shift

The family needs guidance on how to raise the child in accordance with its name and traditions.

Our ideas about ourselves must be in harmony with divine law. This awareness therefore opens the way for wise counsel whether it be from a vision, dreams or intuition.

Explanation of the Dual Shrine

The Elegba/Sebek shrine contains artifacts of categorized energies that governed the birth. At the time of birth cosmic radiation sprayed the earth, like it has always done. This radiation impacts on each and every cell of the child. Science books tell us that the projection of sound initiated creation, which set in motion a spiral, that created the atoms, the elements. Although it happened some 16 billion years ago Cosmic Background Radiation still exists, for it never went away. The name is part of this sound. It is related to this sound. As with much African art/science, it is multilayered and so an actor assists in the explanation of the name and incarnation of the child. Elegba takes the stage with its computational thinking. African epistemology is diverse. It uses binary computers such as Ifa, dreams to give insight, visions and intuition. Researchers (Alamu, Awaorinde and Isharufe 2013) assert that Ifa is a computer system. It uses 256 of odus (scientific verses) to give people insight into human affairs. If an oracle or possessed priest is used the approach is to firstly access information, secondly to stop 'normal' thinking operating and to gain insight into the child's name. This heightened state of mind allows for optimal thinking as the brain is able to deal with a greater quantity of bits of information compared to its normal thinking processes that is extremely limited. Elegba/Sebek, the artistic trickster, is the mathematician and psychologist able to use analytical, analogical and associative thinking strategies.

Guidance to the Family

Guidance should be given to the family on behalf of the child with the community present so that all who are involved with the child's upbringing g are aware of the his/her's mission in life.

The person officiating the naming ceremony should draw upon both ancient and modern literature such a s the Pert Em Hru, Ifa Odu, I Ching and proverbs. This body of literature should also be reinforced with insights that might have come to the traditional African priest, or family member. The priest, using Ifa or I Ching or other divination system is a psychologist and mathematician and from these formulas they can help to plan the child's journey in life.

It is at this point or earlier that the name of the child is whispered in the child's ear and then to the parents. The child now has a name.

For African parents who keep their child in the Eurocentric education system or one based on the nineteenth century European industrial model then their child will leave school or graduate without having attended the most important of all lessons and or lectures, lessons that will have to be delivered by the community. What are these lessons? The first is on Global African Studies which empowers the individual in addressing the immediate and future challenges that their community will face. These modules/lessons mostly mostly be delivered by a team of teachers from the African community themselves. The parent-teacher, the community-teacher, the peer-teacher have to deliver this curriculum but first they have to know it themselves. The curriculum is the African Tree of Knowledge, and its seven components. So what must be taught, when, where and by whom? Below is a summary outline of the Global African Studies and teaching methods that might be considered:

Section 11: Africentric MOOCs

MOOCs stand for Massive Open Online Courses and are an educational delivery system that uses a range of open online resources to provide free or low cost education, typically to students in Higher Education. They are open source platforms that consist of video, assignments, research papers and a learning and management system (LMS). Although they have not been designed for homeschooling as such, many homeschooling families are using open learning environments as part of their blended learning, that is, to supplement their traditional delivery of education. The situation in Africa, as has been noted above, sees many children not going to school not in the same circumstance that a traditional homeschool family would find itself in, due to cost, distance, gender issues and/or security. In such instances MOOCs offers a vital opportunity to provide mass low cost and effective education to African children, and children of the African diaspora. In their article, Massive Open Online Courses for Africa by Africa (2014), Oyo and Kalema identify the challenges that Africa faces when implementing the MOOC strategy that include poor IT infra-structure, poor 24/7 connectivity and week digital literacy in some regions of the continent. However, on the positive side African citizens have a sophisticated use of mobile technology that partly stems from online banking, financial management and a young and dynamic population eager to learn. So MOOCs are able to address Africa's high secondary school age dropout challenge and the high cost of secondary education, which is five times higher than primary education per student.

At Simon Education we have developed an Africentric MOOC (aMOOC) that is a platform with podcasts, videos, lecture notes, research papers, assignments and interactive student exercises. It is a community development resource, a self-development resource, with employment opportunities, training and accreditation resources. It is supported by our online school, home tuition service, apps, study support centres and our education book series, *How to Unlock Your Child's Genius*. This learning and training ecology has more reach than a traditional homeschool environment and accommodates all five teachers that have been mentioned. This open learning environment lends itself to Africa's informal economy where the youth and young people are increasingly seeking self-employment, short qualifications, and training and networking opportunities. This platform, with its branches in the community, empowers the local community who create multiple learning opportunities, resources and take ownership of their children's learning. Moreover it encourages family learning as its "branches" have intergenerational teachers. One of the dangers of MOOCs is that it can lead to cultural imperialism, with the imposition of Eurocentric design, content and pedagogy. Again, we have addressed this by developing an Africentric course to address all these types of issues and promote Indigenous African Knowledge Systems (IAKS). MOOCs could well be the open learning resource that can stop the trend in Africa of former European colonial languages being the dominant language of instruction. aMOOCs can actually be the place where a Pan-African language of instruction is developed.

Final Words

Homeschooling is not a new concept for African people, but it should be combined with vocational education and delivered be multiple teachers who work using one curriculum, the curriculum to unlock the genius of the community in harmony with all other agencies of the universe. We have seen the homeschooling is just a stage in African people seeking to re-create an education system that truly empowers them. This is what Makeda has been seeking and to create a learner in her child that is able to investigate using a variety of methods to help the child become a multi-genius. The tools that she and we need to create our homeschools and other institutions are cultural-scientific tools that our mis-education has suppressed. The challenges that the

African faces today are surmountable. To unlock the genius of the African child and their community, the community must devise their own curriculum, their own teaching and learning methods which should all be informed by their study of their culture.

Index

Accreditation, 52
African civilizations, 31
African researchers, 13
African-Caribbean, 3, 23, 26, 47, 48, 49, 53, 70
Africentric, 36
Apps, 46
Bamun, 40
Bassa, 40
Black African, 12, 31, 36, 37, 49, 68, 74, 80
Black people, 23
Brain, 63
Brain Food, 66
Charlotte Mason Method, 54
Charter School Movement, 26
classroom teacher, 28
community-teacher, 29
Cultural Literacy, 16
curriculum, 3, 5, 10, 12, 23, 25, 26, 27, 28, 29, 30, 34, 38, 39, 41, 49, 54, 57, 60, 69, 80, 81
Digital Badge, 52
Eclectic Method, 54
Edo, 40
Education Research, 26
Educational Design, 48
Employment Trends, 58
Family Model, 53
family-centered, 30
Global African Studies, 13, 16, 48, 49, 50, 55, 59, 68, 80
Hieroglyphic, 41
Home Learning Profile, 34
homeschool movement, 3, 13, 36, 46, 52, 55
Hybrid Model, 53
Independent Schools, 26
industrial model, 24
Jenne, 13, 55
John Holt, 3, 26, 54, 61
kinaesthetic learning, 13
Kukakui, 40
Mandombe, 40

Melanin, 63
Mende, 40
Metu Neter, 40
Mobile Education, 44, 45, 46
Mobile Education: Apps, 44
Move-2- Genius, 62
N'Ko, 40
Naming Ceremony, 70
Nsibidi, 40
Online education, 46
online learning, 47
oware, 41
Pan-Africanist, 4
parent-teacher, 29
Peer-teacher, 29
poverty gap, 30
Prussian influence, 27
Questionnaire, 10
Reading, 44
sedentary learning, 13
Shrine, 79
Simon Education, 1, 3, 23, 26, 28, 29, 47, 50
Simon Method, 53
Socratic Method, 54
Steiner, 3, 10, 26
Studies Method, 54
supplementary movement, 31
The Co-operative Model, 53
The Home School Movement, 26
The Merotic, 40
The Supplementary School Movement, 26
Tifinagh, 40
Timbuktu, 13, 55
Trends in Employment, 57
unemployment, 30
Unschooling Method, 54
violence trap, 30
virtual-teacher, 29
wealth gap, 30
writing systems, 40

African researchers, 13
African-Caribbean, 3, 14, 17, 18, 40, 46, 49, 50, 73

Black African, 12, 22, 28, 29, 49, 50, 71, 77
curriculum, 4, 5, 10, 12, 14, 16, 17, 19, 20, 21, 22, 26, 30, 31, 33, 41, 50, 54, 56, 71, 83

Global African Studies, 13, 42, 49, 50, 56, 57, 71
homeschool movement, 3, 13, 28, 42, 44, 52
Jenne, 13, 42
John Holt, 3, 17, 41, 64

Pan-Africanist, 4
Questionnaire, 10
Steiner, 3, 10, 17
Timbuktu, 13, 42

Selected bibliography

Ali, Mosaraf: and Brar, Jiwan. 2002. *Therapeutic Yoga*. Vermilion.

Apple, Michael. 1995. *Education and Power*. Routledge

Dryden, Gordon: and Vos Jeanette. 2001. *The learning Revolution*. Network Educational Press Limited.

Enkamit, Hehi Metu Ra. 1993. *African Names*. Ser Ap-uat Publishers.

Hannaford, Carla. 1995. *Smart Moves, Why Learning is Not All in The Head*. Great Ocean Publishers.

Holford, Patrick. 1997. *The Optimum Nutrition Bible*: Piatkus Ltd.

Holt, John. *How Children Fail*. 1984. How Children Fail: Pelican Books.

Liebeck, Pamela. 1984. *How Children Learn Mathematics:* Pelican Books Litd.

McCabe, Des. 2011. *Work it Out*: Hay House.

McGuinness, Diane. 1997. *Why Children Can't Read*: Penguin Books. McGuinness & McGuinness, Carmen & Geoffrey. 1998. *Reading Reflex*: Penguin.

Mindell, Earl. 2001. *The Vitamin Bible*. Arlington Books.

Moore, T Owens. 1995. The Science of Melanin, Dispelling the Myths: Beckham House Publishers.

Montessori, Maria. 1991. *The Advanced Montessori Method - 1*: Clio Press. Mukerjea, Dilip. 1996. *Superbrain*: Oxford University Press.

Ratey, John. 2004. *A User's Guide to the Brain*: Abacus.

Simon, David. 2008. *How to Unlock Your Child's Genius*: Simon Education.

Simon, David. 2012. *How to Unlock Your Family's Genius*: Simon Education.

Wilson, Amos. 1991. *Awakening the Natural Genius of Black Children*: Afrikan World Infosystems.

MOTORCYCLE
RIDERS HUB

MODULE 1 COURSE

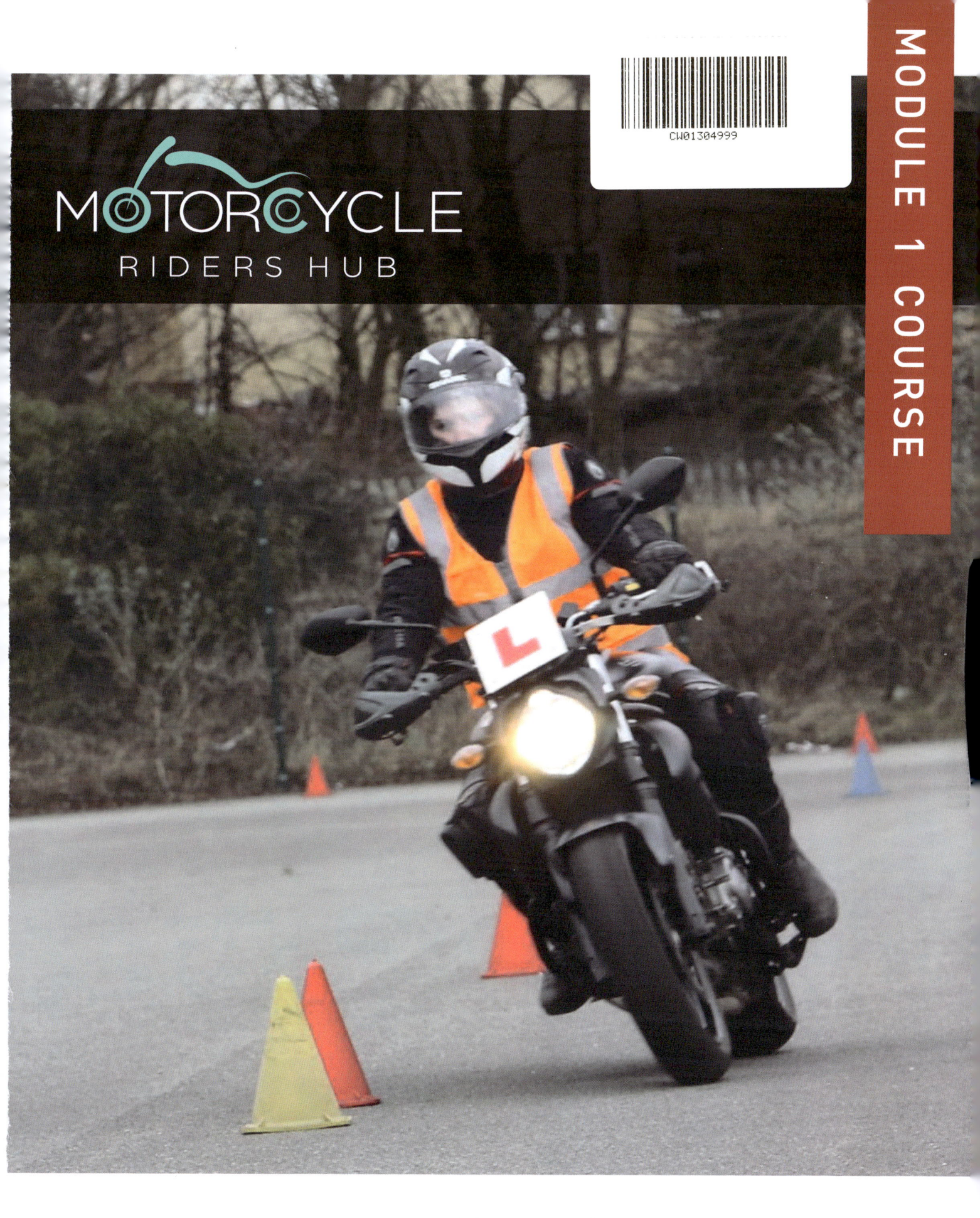

KEEP IT ON THE BLACK STUFF

MotorcycleRidersHub.co.uk

© MOTORCYCLE RIDERS HUB

First published May 2021

The contents of the Motorcycle Riders Hub Module 1 Course e-book are copyright © Motorcycle Riders Hub and must not be reproduced or distributed in any form, without express permission in writing with consent from Motorcycle Riders Hub.

The information contained in this e-book is accurate at the time of publication.

This e-book is intended to be used alongside the corresponding Motorcycle Riders Hub Academy and professional motorcycle training.

Use this document as a guide and learning platform to help enhance skills and knowledge. Use of this e-book is subject to Motorcycle Riders Hub terms and conditions.

KEEP IT ON THE BLACK STUFF

ABOUT SIMON HAYES

A full time instructor since 1991, Simon Hayes is a highly experienced motorcycle instructor and well known within the industry. Simon's first six years as an instructor were spent teaching military personnel, where he had a 100% success rate and earned a reputation for high level training.

Since 1996 Simon has operated a respected multisite motorcycle training business covering Birmingham and the Midlands. Over thirty years of dedication to the highest possible standards of motorcycle training has forged a reputation for excellence. Simon has seen many changes and challenges affecting the industry, his own training school has continued to thrive and develop.

Over these decades Simon has covered over a million miles and personally delivered novice to advanced training to many thousands of bikers. Simon is also sought after UK wide as an accomplished instructor trainer and has introduced countless new motorcycle instructors to the sector. In addition, Simon maintains a busy diary of European Tours covering advanced riding on the continent, off road training, track day training, local club and charity rides.

Some years ago, Simon began to improve his students motorcycle training experience through complimentary video based training.

Through pre-course learning students are able to visualise motorcycle skills training and find that their practical training is greatly enhanced.

Over a ten year period, these video training resources were refined, resulting in a first edition being formally published and more widely available.

KEEP IT ON THE BLACK STUFF

ABOUT SIMON HAYES CONTINUED...

From starting video training on a DVD, the delivery has been changed and nurtured into Motorcycle Riders Hub, the UK's first 100% video based motorcycle training resource. As the founder of Motorcycle Riders Hub, Simon's vision is to enhance rider training and safety across the UK, empowering both new and experienced riders to continually improve their skills.

Simon believes that the Motorcycle Riders Hub resources should not be used in isolation and must not be viewed as a substitute for professional motorcycle training. To get the best out of the training resource, riders should use the video training and practical training in conjunction to elevate their learning experience. Practical training alone does not give learner riders all the tools they need.

Motorcycle Riders Hub is supported by a number of full time trainers and other professional motorcyclists, as well as an Advisory Panel, they are all committed to road safety and the values of 'Keep it on the black stuff'.

As Motorcycle Riders Hub continues to develop, its aim is to give riders a useful dedicated e-learning platform. Simon's ambition is to reach as many new riders as possible countrywide to help and guide them to become better riders, his commitment to motorcycle training continues with an ongoing full schedule of practical courses.

Motorcycle Riders Hub
Keep it on the black stuff

KEEP IT ON THE BLACK STUFF

ABOUT MOTORCYCLE RIDERS HUB

Over the decades there has been significant changes made to motorcycle training. The latest development in rider training saw the introduction and implementation of CBT, Module 1 and Module 2 motorcycle tests. The result has been a substantial uplift in learner riders skills and ability.

Our vision is to help learner riders at all levels to improve their knowledge, ability and skills by using an online e-learning platform to raise personal riding standards.

Motorcycle Riders Hub is the UK's only 100% online motorcycle video training resource helping learner riders through their Compulsory Basic Training (CBT), Direct Access, Module 1 and Module 2 motorcycle tests.

The online program of dedicated guidance and learning resources will help all riders to develop and enhance their skills, ensuring they are better and safer riders and can keep it on the black stuff.

KEEP IT ON THE BLACK STUFF

CONTENTS

Getting ready for Module 1

1. Learning to ride — 6
2. About Module 1 — 7
3. Course explained — 8
4. What to take — 9
5. What to wear — 10
6. Examiners briefing — 11
7. Module 1 test area — 12
8. Rider faults and fails — 14

The Module 1 test exercise *

9. Entering the test centre — 15
10. Parking up — 16
11. Manual handling — 17
12. Slalom and figure-of-eight — 18
13. Slow control — 19
14. U-turn — 20
15. Riding the circuit — 21
16. Controlled stop — 22
17. Emergency stop — 24
18. Avoidance exercise — 26
19. Leaving the test centre — 28

What's next

20. Take responsibility — 29
21. Now for Module 2 — 30

Note

The Module 1 motorcycle test has a left and right hand circuit. During the Module 1 test candidates will only complete the test in one direction.

The training notes only show and reference the left hand circuit. The right hand circuit is exactly the same in the opposite direction

KEEP IT ON THE BLACK STUFF

LEARNING TO RIDE

Biking is a fabulous pastime, people are learning to ride a motorcycle for economic reasons. On the whole, motorcycles are less expensive to purchase, tax and insure than cars. Taking account of the cost of learning, they offer a cheaper route to getting mobile.

Motorbikes can be a faster way to travel, which means riders will not get frustrated with traffic congestion. Given these benefits, there is also a good case for motorcycles as a greener mode of transport, especially in towns and cities with electric motorcycles.

Riders must recognise and take responsibility for their own vulnerability on the roads. This requires an investment in good protective clothing, plus a commitment to take part in compulsory and ongoing motorcycle training.

Compulsory Basic Training (CBT) is a starting point. It sets the minimum standard for new riders, allowing them to ride unaccompanied on the road, it is the lowest level of rider skill and rider safety.

Taking further training to pass the Module 1 and 2 tests are just a start on the riding ladder. Seeking professional training and guidance will be an advantage to pave the way for the Module 1 test. It is essential to know what the criteria is prior to turning up at the test centre for the Module 1 test.

Module 1 tests take place around the UK at a purpose built Motorcycle Manoeuvring Areas (MMA). The Module 1 test assesses that a rider is safe and has sufficient control of a motorcycle.

The Module 1 test includes a variety of slow-control manoeuvres, manual handling and high speed exercises.

Although there are some subtle variations, each MMA is identical. One difference can be the position of the entry gates, which can vary from site to site. Each site is identical in size, high friction tarmac surface, cone position and the overall dimensions.

KEEP IT ON THE BLACK STUFF

ABOUT MODULE 1

Module 1 tests take place throughout the UK at a network of purpose built Motorcycle Manoeuvring Areas (MMA). The Module 1 test assesses that a rider is safe and has sufficient control of the motorcycle to proceed to the Module 2 test.

The Module 1 test includes a variety of slow control manoeuvres, manual handling and high-speed exercises.

Whilst there are some subtle variations, each Motorcycle Manoeuvring Area (Module 1 test area) is identical. One difference can be the position of the entry gates, which can vary from site to site.

Each site is identical in size, road surface (high friction tarmac), cone position and the overall dimensions of each exercise.

In order to book a Module 1 test you must have a valid driving licence, a Compulsory Basic Training (CBT) and theory test certificates, both must be in date.

Although Module 1 tests can be booked directly with the DVSA, it is advisable to book Module 1 training (including the test) through a local motorcycle training school.

Module 1 training should result in much higher levels of preparation, confidence, skill and safety. Statistics show that there are higher first time pass rates when candidates have taken a professional training approach.

Instructor Tip

"Always choose a training provider that uses the actual test centre for pre test practice."

KEEP IT ON THE BLACK STUFF

COURSE EXPLAINED

The Motorcycle Riders Hub Module 1 Course does not substitute professional motorcycle training. It has been structured to enhance the skills and knowledge gained through Module 1 training when delivered by qualified motorcycle instructors.

For candidates embarking on Module 1 training for the first time, there is a lot to take in. This is especially true for those with limited riding experience. Motorcycle Riders Hub does not recommend a DIY approach to Module 1 motorcycle training.

The Module 1 Course has been put together by a team of highly experienced, skilled and qualified motorcycle instructors. It has been further enhanced through candidate feedback and endorsed by independent professional motorcyclists.

Content includes:

- Instructional training videos
- Complete Module 1 mock tests
- Podcasts for each training exercise
- e-books showing exercise diagrams
- Progress check tests
- Instructor tips

The aim of the Module 1 Course is to make the test easier which creates more confident and safer riders. The course enhances a candidate's Module 1 training experience through pre-learning and the opportunity to experience, visualise and internalise the actual Module 1 Course.

Candidates can watch the Module 1 videos as many times as they like. Plus listen to podcasts, read the e-books and complete the progress tests. The outcome is a better prepared, less stressed experience.

Candidates who know what is coming will have a better mind set and will be better prepared as they go through each exercise during the practical test. Having an understanding of how to safely navigate the slow control and speed exercises prepares for success and is a step closer to a full licence.

KEEP IT ON THE BLACK STUFF

WHAT TO TAKE

Prior preparation is essential, don't leave getting things ready until the last minute or overlook the required Module 1 test paperwork. Failure to provide the correct documents will result in a cancelled Module 1 test and loss of test fee.

Mandatory requirements:

▶ Compulsory Basic Training (CBT)

The CBT certificate must be in date and correctly filled out

▶ UK driving licence

Current full or provisional UK photocard driving licence (photographs are valid for 10 years)
Address should be correct (current address)
For paper licence holders (no photocard) a valid UK passport is required

▶ Theory test certificate

In date and valid motorcycle theory test pass certificate (Valid for two years from date of issue)

▶ Motorcycle

The correct engine size for test being undertaken
Road legal - MOT if required
Taxed and Insured
Full sized L Plates on the front and rear

▶ Don't be late

There are no allowances for being late and missing a test booking will result in a lost test fee

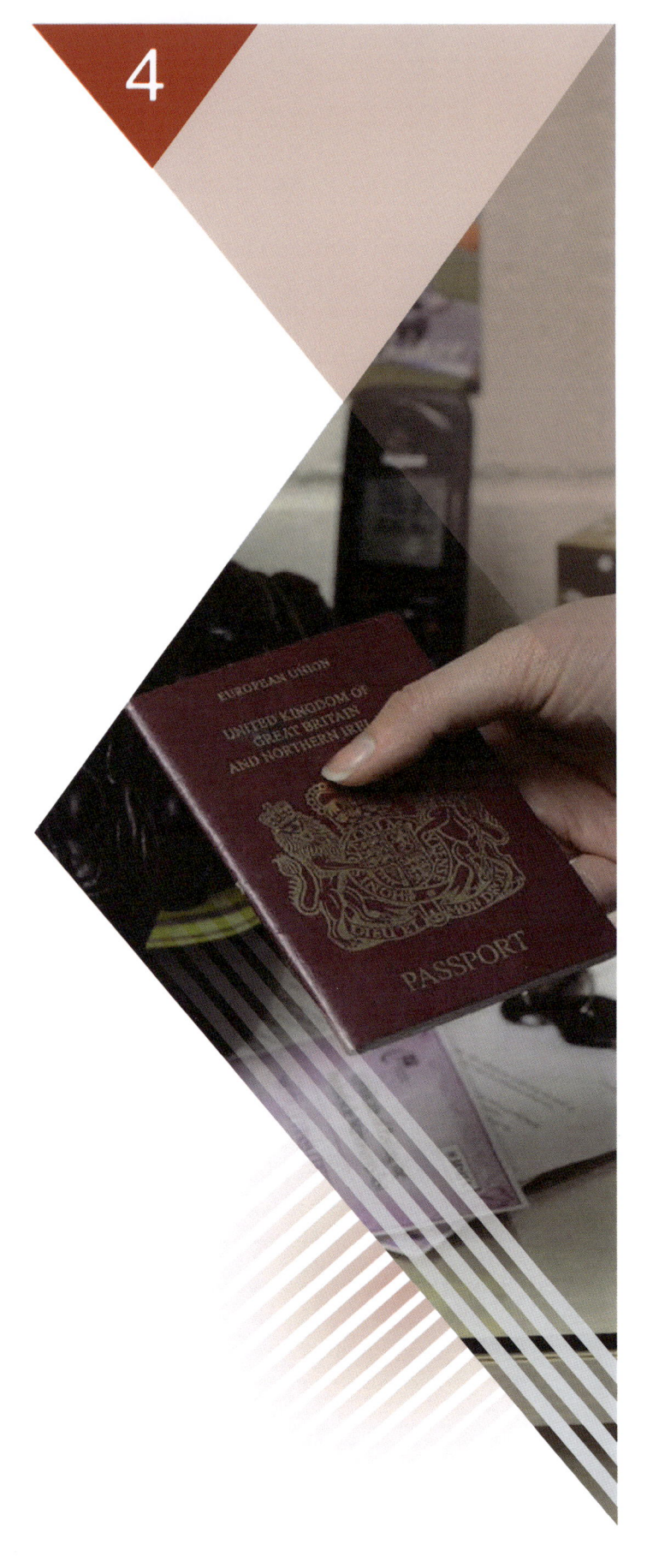

KEEP IT ON THE BLACK STUFF

WHAT TO WEAR

Although it is not a mandatory test requirement, it is advised that appropriate protective clothing is worn.

This should include leather motorcycle boots that provide a good level of ankle protection, along with armoured textile or leather motorcycle trousers and jacket.

These should be worn with a motorcycle helmet that meets the correct safety standards, plus quality motorcycle gloves and a high visibility vest.

Minimum acceptable clothing requirements:
(if not wearing purpose made motorcycle clothing)

- ▶ Motorcycle helmet: that meets the required safety standards
- ▶ Sturdy footwear: must support and protect ankles
- ▶ Denim trousers: heavy denim (no holes/tears or fashion jeans)
- ▶ Denim jacket: heavy denim (no holes/tears), with several layers worn underneath
- ▶ Motorcycle gloves: good quality and condition

Instructor Tips

"Put everything out the night before, including documents. So that you pick everything up on the way out the house and don't forget anything."

"Wearing the right clothing means you're less likely to need hospital treatment if you are involved in an accident."

KEEP IT ON THE BLACK STUFF

EXAMINERS BRIEFING

With sufficient practice and an adequate number of lessons prior to the Module 1 test, candidates can be fully prepared and know what to expect.

30 minutes is allocated for each Module 1 test and only about 15 minutes is required within the Motorcycle Manoeuvring Area, there is no time pressure and no need to rush.

The examiner's briefing will be straightforward and to the point. General instructions include:

1) don't hit any cones
2) carry out all relevant safety observations

With the aid of a diagram, the examiner will explain the requirements of each Module 1 exercise. If a manoeuvre is attempted, but clearly misunderstood, the examiner may invite a second attempt.

Where mandatory speed requirements are not met (emergency stop and avoidance exercise) a second attempt will generally be given.

If asked, the examiners will advise the measured speed on the first attempt. This can help candidates to reach the required speed on their second attempt.

KEEP IT ON THE BLACK STUFF

MODULE 1 TEST AREA

LEFT CIRCUIT DIAGRAM
USED BY EXAMINER TO EXPLAIN THE TEST

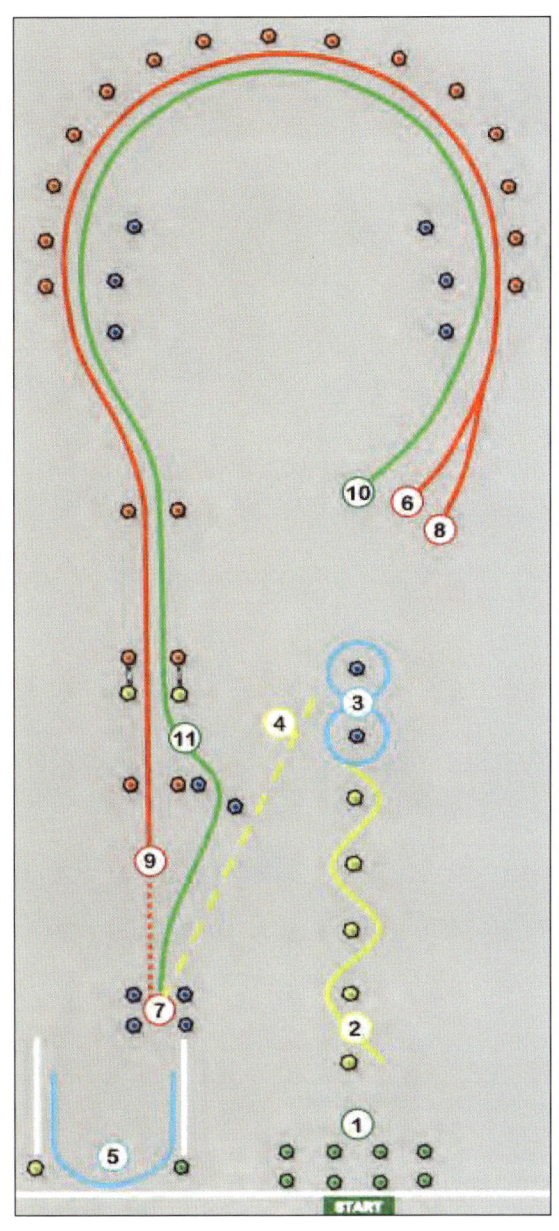

1. Stands and handling
2. Slalom
3. Figure-of-eight
4. Slow ride
5. U-turn
6. Cornering
7. Controlled stop
8. Circuit ride
9. Emergency brake
10. Circuit ride
11. Avoidance

Diagram for illustrative purposes only and is not exactly to scale. See later chapters for the specifics of each exercise and speed requirements.

KEEP IT ON THE BLACK STUFF

MODULE 1 TEST AREA CONTINUED...

RIGHT CIRCUIT DIAGRAM
USED BY EXAMINER TO EXPLAIN THE TEST

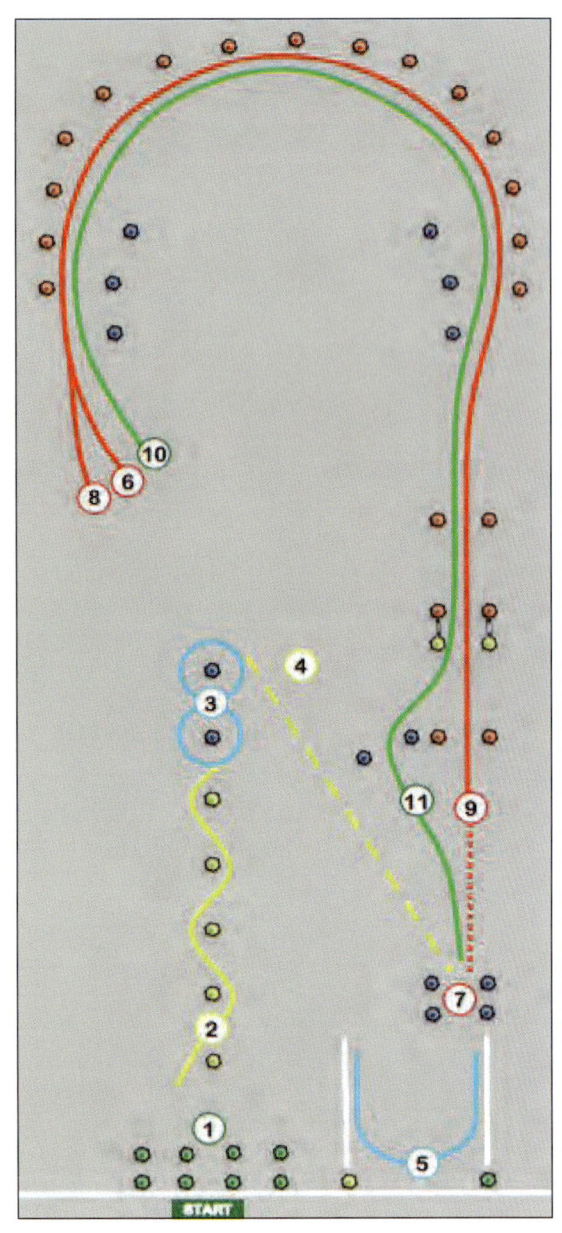

1. Stands and handling
2. Slalom
3. Figure-of-eight
4. Slow ride
5. U-turn
6. Cornering
7. Controlled stop
8. Circuit ride
9. Emergency brake
10. Circuit ride
11. Avoidance

Diagram for illustrative purposes only and is not exactly to scale. See later chapters for the specifics of each exercise and speed requirements.

KEEP IT ON THE BLACK STUFF

RIDER FAULTS AND FAILS

Candidates are allowed up to five minor rider faults that do not impact on safety. Minor faults can include missed gear changes and stalling. Being too slow for the emergency stop and/or the avoidance exercise could also count as a minor fault.

Missed observations can be minor faults, but if safety dictates can be recorded as major faults, resulting in a fail. Five or less non serious faults would result in a Module 1 pass.

More than five minor faults will result in a failed attempt. One major fault will also result in a fail and in most cases, too many missed observations will also result in a failure. Major faults are usually rider errors that could present danger to the rider or other road users.

Major faults can include:

- Too many missed observations
- Putting a foot down during an exercise to prevent the bike falling over
- Making contact with cones
- Failing to complete a manoeuvre
- Failing to reach a mandatory speed
- An uncontrolled/dangerous skid
- Failing to stop in the correct place
- Taking too long to stop on the emergency stop

In the event of a dangerous fault or unsafe riding, the examiner could stop the test. Candidates are advised to continue and not to assume the worst or keep their own score.

Instructor Tip

"If you make a mistake, try to forget about it. Keep going and don't convince yourself that you have failed.

There are plenty who think they have failed, only to be awarded a pass certificate."

KEEP IT ON THE BLACK STUFF

ENTERING THE TEST CENTRE

The Module 1 test begins as soon as the candidate is handed over to the examiner. This is when the test assessments start.

At all times act as if on a public road, ensuring that road safety observations are constantly being carried out. Listen carefully to the examiner and always ask for clarification if needed.

The candidate will be invited to enter the Motorcycle Manoeuvring Area and to stop just inside the gates. Listen carefully, take your time and do not rush.

To enter the Motorcycle Manoeuvring Area:

- Sit on the bike
- Start the bike and select 1st gear
- Carry out rear observations and if safe, ride into the test centre
- Stop where indicated and select neutral
- Await further instructions from the examiner

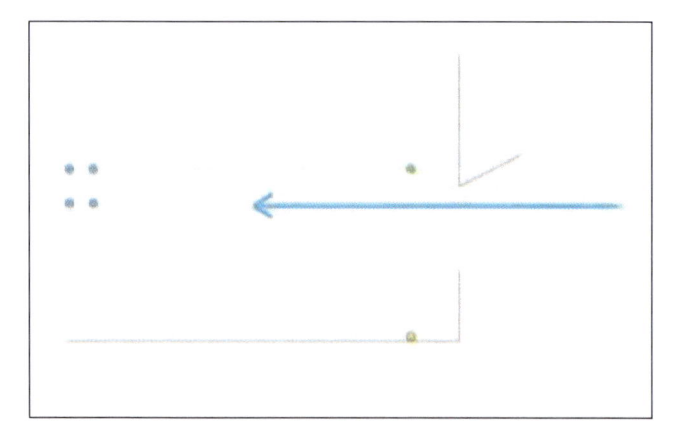

Diagram: Entering Motorcycle Manoeuvring Area

KEEP IT ON THE BLACK STUFF

PARKING UP

The gates will be closed and the candidate will be asked to ride and park the bike in a parking bay, facing the fence, in one of the two parking bays (marked by four green cones).

Candidates are advised to think about the exercise first, remain calm and not to rush. The examiner will already be making assessments.

Not rushing to park up can help to settle test nerves, giving time to view the test centre, position of marker cones and general layout.

To park up in the parking bay:

▶ Select 1st gear and carry out rear observations

▶ Look and ride forward, riding a large arc to help position the motorcycle

▶ Ensure the bike is straight in the parking bay

▶ Stop and select neutral

▶ Turn engine off and put the bike onto the stand

▶ Dismount and await further instructions

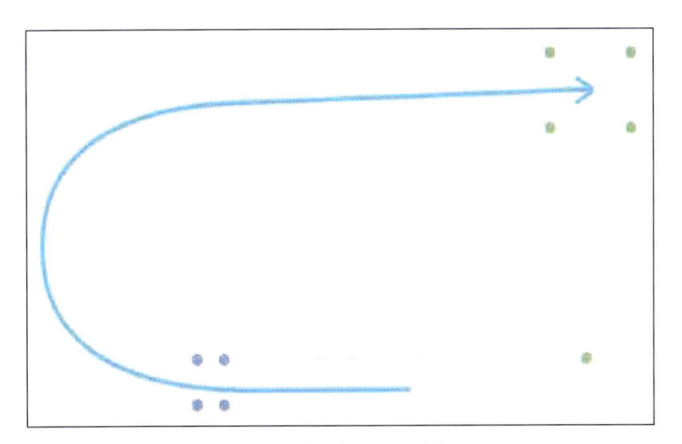

Diagram: Parking up (left circuit)

KEEP IT ON THE BLACK STUFF

MANUAL HANDLING

The motorcycle must be wheeled to the opposite parking bay. This can be achieved by pushing the bike back in a semi-circle or by walking the bike straight back, then forward in a semi-circle, then back into the opposite parking bay.

Do not rush. Carry out safety observations and look in the direction of travel. Avoid parking at an awkward angle, ensure the side stand is up before moving the bike. Use the front brake as required and take your time.

Nb. A side stand is easier to use than a centre stand.

To carry out this manual handling exercise:

▶ Take the bike off the stand

▶ Hand on the back seat and push the bike backwards in a straight line

▶ Look in the direction of travel

▶ Use front brake as required

▶ Ensure the bike is straight in the opposite parking bay

▶ Put the bike safely on to the stand and await further instruction.

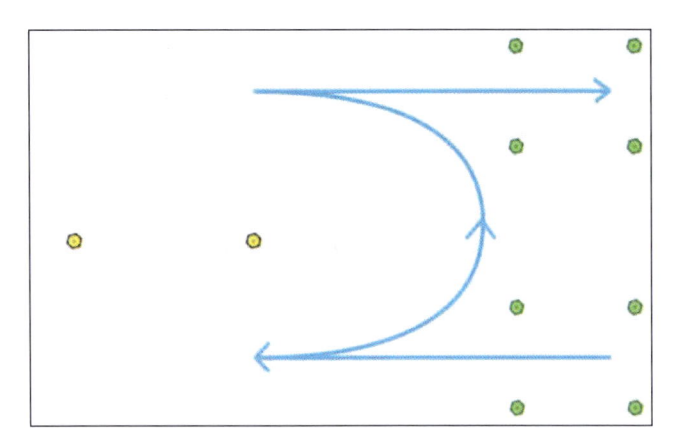

Diagram: Manual handling (left circuit)

KEEP IT ON THE BLACK STUFF

SLALOM AND FIGURE-OF-EIGHT

For this exercise candidates should use the throttle, clutch control and rear brake. Adequate revs to prevent stalling and a steady speed are essential.

Candidates should keep their focus as far ahead as possible, rather than on the closest cone. The slalom is around the five yellow cones. The figure-of-eight then follows around the two blue cones. Prior training with a professional motorcycle instructor is crucial.

Steering wide in the figure-of-eight reduces the risk of putting a foot down. During this whole exercise, candidates should avoid using the front brake.

To carry out the slalom and figure-of-eight:

▶ Sit on the bike, remove the stand and start up

▶ Select 1st gear and carry out rear observations

▶ Ride forward using slow control

▶ Look ahead through the course

▶ Slalom between yellow cones

▶ Two figure-of-eight around blue cones

▶ Do not ride tight circles, go as wide as required

▶ When instructed, ride out of the exercise

▶ Select neutral and await further instructions

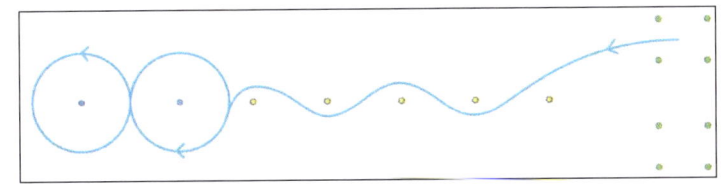

Diagram: slalom and figure of eight (left circuit)

KEEP IT ON THE BLACK STUFF

SLOW CONTROL

This walking pace slow ride assesses a candidate's balance as well as their control of the rear brake, throttle and clutch.

This exercise simulates the skills required to ride safely in slow moving traffic and in other slow control scenarios. It is important to look ahead, whilst keeping the revs up, slip the clutch and lightly use the rear brake to keep the speed at a walking pace. A light grip of the handle bars and gripping the fuel tank with the knees can aid rider balance.

The examiner will watch from behind. The candidate should keep their focus ahead and not use the front brake. Stop the bike at the beginning of the U-turn exercise area near the four blue cones.

To carry out the slow control ride:

- ▶ Select 1st gear and carry out rear observations
- ▶ Ride forward and focus ahead
- ▶ Ride at a walking pace
- ▶ Use throttle, clutch and rear brake
- ▶ Do not use the front brake
- ▶ Approach blue cones straight
- ▶ Stop, select neutral and await further instructions from the examiner

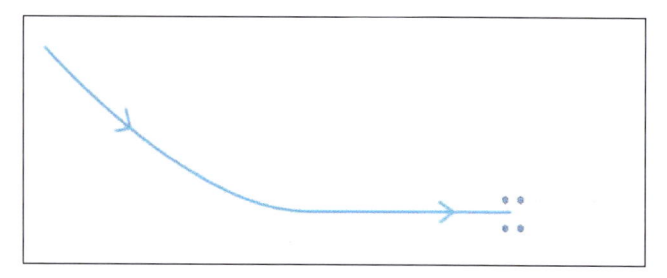

Diagram: Slow control ride (left circuit)

KEEP IT ON THE BLACK STUFF

U-TURN

This slow control exercise requires good balance and effective use of the throttle, clutch and rear brake.

Starting from near the four blue cones, the rider must turn the bike around as if on a public road i.e. with due care, without hitting the white lines (simulating the kerb) and without putting a foot down on the floor.

The U-turn must remain within the white lines, with the bike coming to a stop, adjacent to where the exercise started, facing in the opposite direction. The key is to keep the head up, look in the direction of travel and not to look down.

To complete the U-turn:

- Select 1st gear and carry out rear observations
- Right shoulder check last (as if on the public road)
- Look forward and ride parallel to the white line
- Midway along line, carry out a right hand life saver
- Ensure the bike is near the white line prior to turning
- At centre of turn, look to the right and down the line
- Stop at the end of the white line
- Select neutral and await further instructions

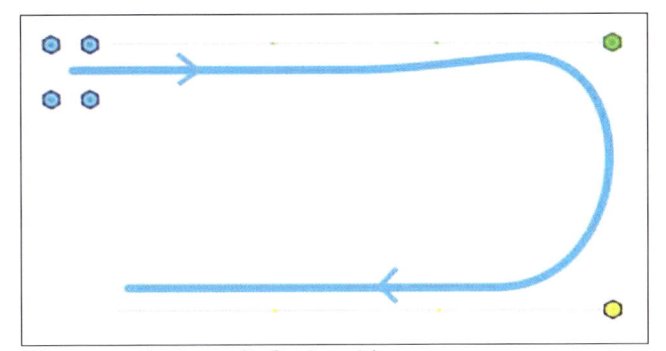

Diagram: U-turn (left circuit)

Instructor Tip

"Make sure the front wheel is near the white line before starting the turn."

KEEP IT ON THE BLACK STUFF

RIDING THE CIRCUIT

There are three riding the circuit exercises, they are:

1) Controlled stop
2) Emergency stop
3) Avoidance exercise

Common factors shared by all three exercises:

▶ Select 1st gear and carry out rear observations

▶ Riding towards curve, select 2nd gear (max 20mph)

▶ Avoid braking in the curve (maintain 19mph)

▶ Entering the curve, aim for 1 metre from red cones

▶ Two cones past the centre cone, turn towards blue cones

▶ On exit from curve, aim for 1 metre from blue cones

▶ Avoid target fixation on the cones. Look up and ahead for a safe and correct exit from the circuit.

Speed requirements

Controlled stop
Curve: 19mph (30km/h) - advised
Speed camera: >30mph (>48km/h) - advised

Emergency stop
Curve: 19mph (30km/h) no camera - required
Speed camera: 32mph (50km/h) - required

Avoidance
Curve: 19mph (30km/h) no camera - required
Speed camera: 32mph (50km/h) - required

Instructor Tip

"Practice makes perfect, try to find a training school that hires the test centre for practice."

KEEP IT ON THE BLACK STUFF

CONTROLLED STOP

The controlled stop is the first of the speed exercises and has no mandatory speed requirements. Riding towards the curve at no more than 20 mph should prevent the need to brake which will help with positioning, both in the curve and on exiting.

Avoid looking directly at the cones, but keep them in peripheral vision. Look up and ahead through the corner and then down the course in the direction of the four blue cones. Do not use excessive speed and no higher than 2nd gear (depending on the motorcycle being used).

To carry out the controlled stop exercise:

- Select 1st gear and carry out rear observations
- Look and ride forward. 2nd gear and 20 mph
- In curve, position 1 metre from red cones
- At centre point, look for 2nd cone (as a guide)
- Turn towards blue cones to straighten up the exit
- Accelerate towards speed camera
- At first red cones close throttle
- At speed camera, start braking using both brakes
- Approaching blue cones use the rear brake only and select 1st gear
- Stop with front wheel inside the area designated by the four blue cones
- Once stopped, go into neutral and await further instruction from the examiner

Instructor Tip

"Stopping with the front wheel outside the box of blue cones will result in test failure.

Imagine you are stopping at the end of a road and there is a white line between the two last cones."

KEEP IT ON THE BLACK STUFF

CONTROLLED STOP CONTINUED...

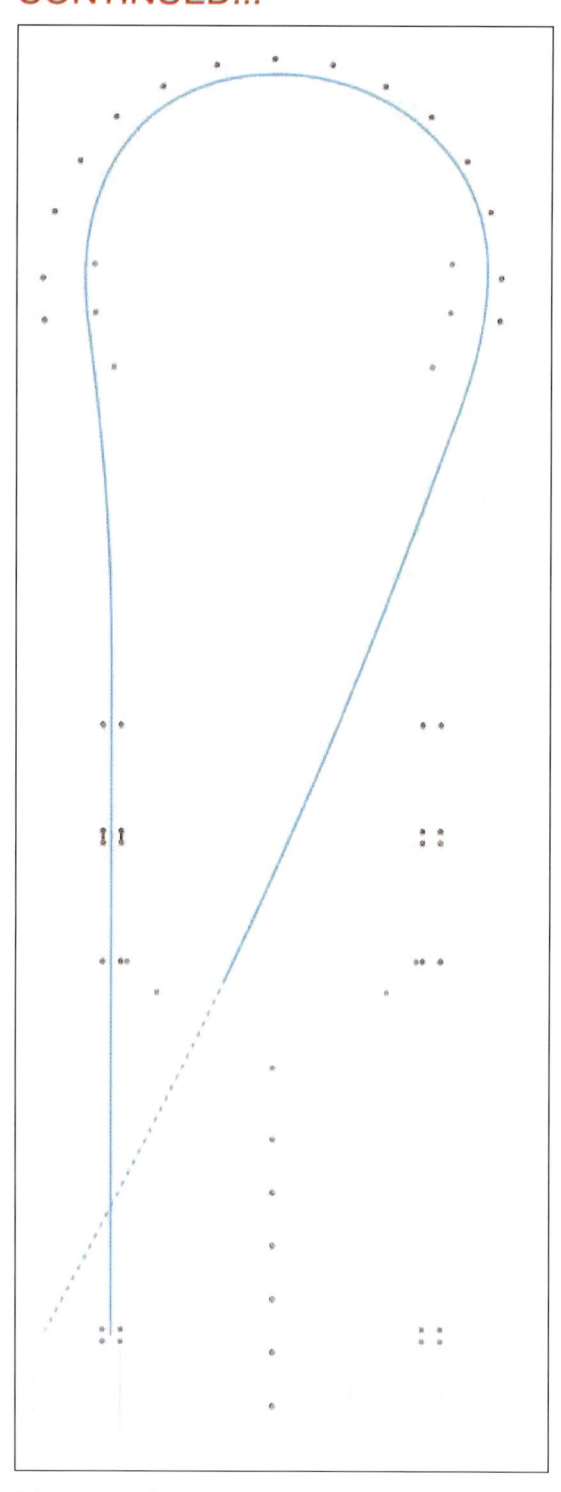

Diagram: Controlled stop (left circuit)

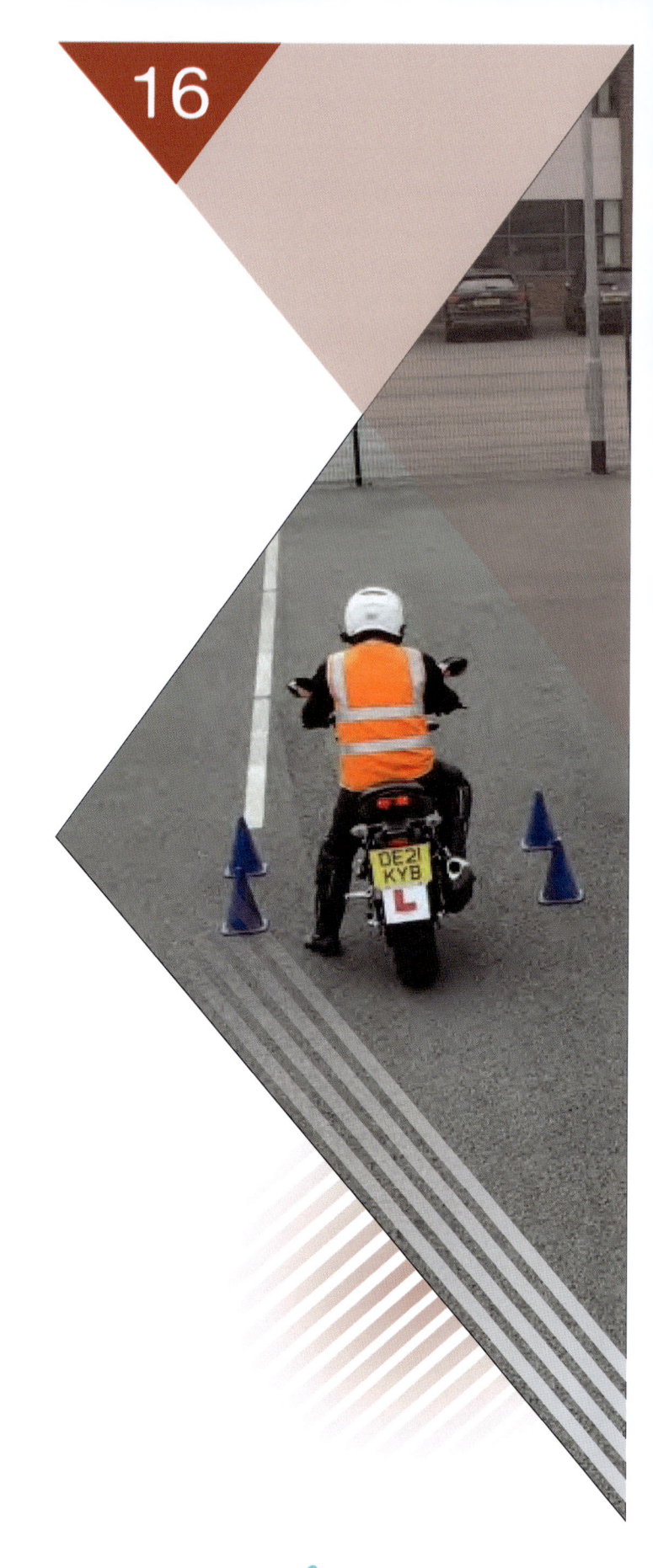

16

KEEP IT ON THE BLACK STUFF

EMERGENCY STOP

With the emergency stop, the speed requirements are: 19mph (30kmh) in the curve and 32mph (50kmh) at the speed camera.

The candidate should ride towards the curve at 20mph. This reduces the need to brake and makes it easier to line up in the best position during and exiting the circuit. Look up, ahead and use peripheral vision to locate the cones position. Exiting the curve, look down the site and towards the four blue cones.

Be aware of how the weather may affect braking and stopping distances. Ensure that this exercise has been thoroughly practiced. Sometimes a second attempt will be allowed if the candidate fails to reach the required speed.

To carry out the emergency stop:

- Select 1st gear and carry out rear observations
- Look and ride forward. 2nd gear with a max speed of 20mph
- In the curve, position 1 metre from red cones
- Avoid braking and maintain 19mph in the circuit
- At the centre point, look for the 2nd cone away (as a guide)
- Turn towards blue cones to straighten up the exit
- Accelerate and maintain at least 32mph
- Examiner will raise their hand to start the emergency stop
- Power off and carry out an emergency stop
- Once stopped, select 1st and await instructions
- Examiner may instruct you to move forward
- When the bike is in 1st gear, carry out observations and move forward
- Stop where requested, select neutral and await further instructions from the examiner

KEEP IT ON THE BLACK STUFF

EMERGENCY STOP CONTINUED...

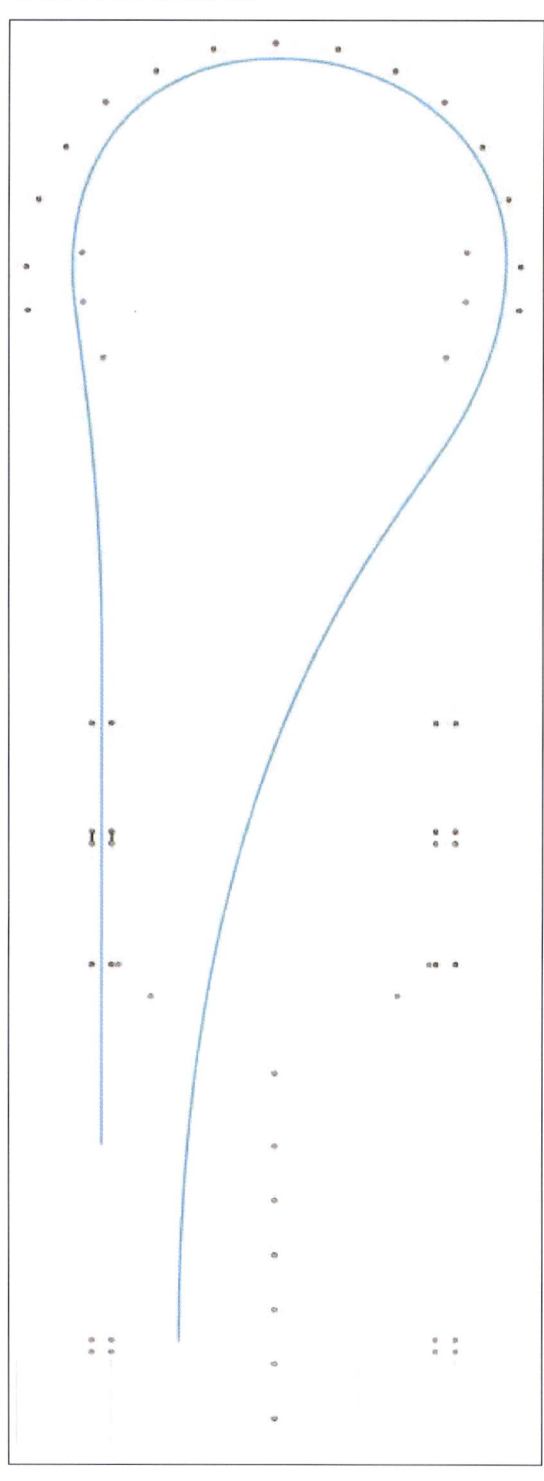

17

Diagram: Emergency stop (left circuit)

KEEP IT ON THE BLACK STUFF

AVOIDANCE EXERCISE

The final speed exercise is the avoidance. The key to this exercise is practice. It is generally accepted that 2nd gear is best and works well for most bikes. When exiting the circuit accelerate to 35mph, then close the throttle at the first set of red cones. This transfers the weight to the front wheel, which aids counter steering and results in a speed of 32mph at the speed camera.

It is vital to look between and beyond the two blue avoidance cones and not to focus on the first one. After the avoidance, gently steer back, lightly applying the rear brake and when straight and upright, use both brakes. Do not use the front brake while the bike is not upright. A second attempt is generally allowed if the candidate fails to reach the required speed

To carry out the avoidance exercise:

- Select 1st gear and carry out rear observations
- Look and ride forward in 2nd gear at 20mph
- In the circuit, position 1 metre from the red cones
- Avoid braking and maintain 19mph in the circuit
- At centre point, look for the 2nd cone away (as guide)
- Turn towards blue cones to straighten up the exit
- Accelerate and maintain 35mph
- At the first set of red cones turn the power off
- Go through speed camera at 32mph (50kmh)
- Look between the two blue cones
- Swerve through the two blue avoidance cones
- Look and steer towards blue cones at the end of the course
- Lightly apply rear brake to slow down after swerving through the first blue cones
- When bike straightens up, apply the front brake
- Stop between blue cones at the end of the course
- Select neutral and await further instructions from the examiner

KEEP IT ON THE BLACK STUFF

AVOIDANCE EXERCISE CONTINUED...

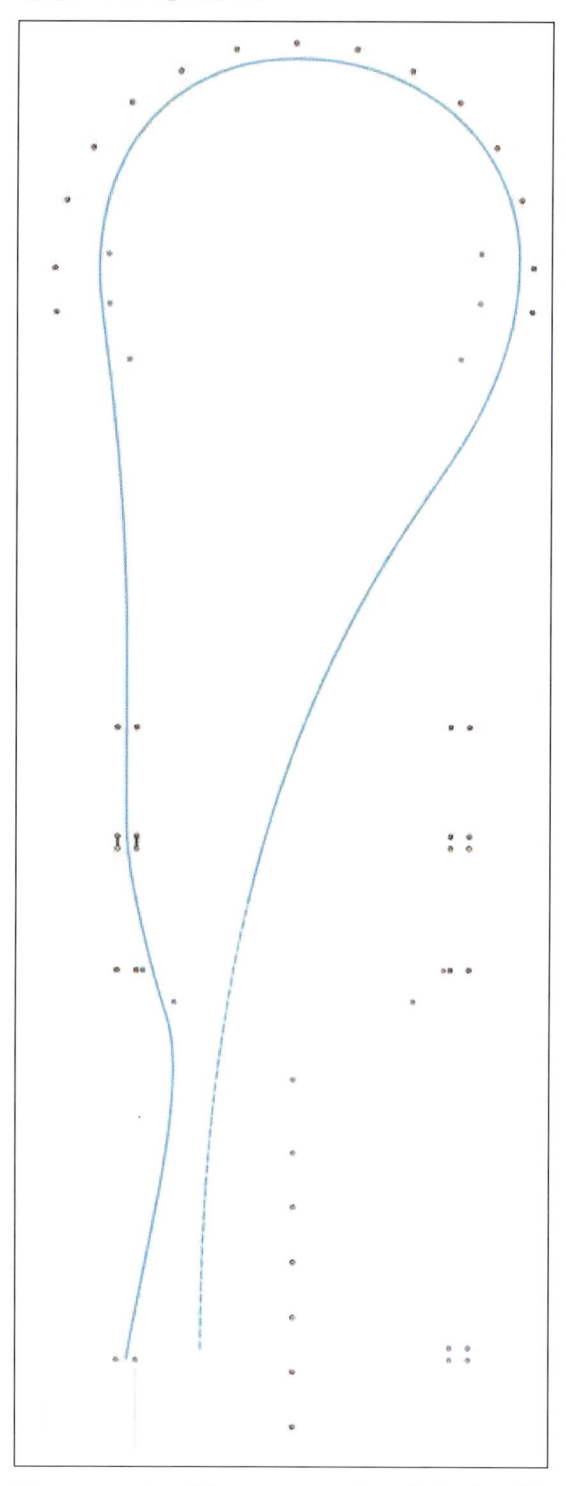

Diagram: Avoidance exercise (left circuit)

KEEP IT ON THE BLACK STUFF

LEAVING THE TEST CENTRE

The Module 1 test ends when the candidate leaves the Motorcycle Manoeuvring Area and parks up (outside the gates). The examiner continues making assessments and there is still room for mistakes.

Candidates must avoid rushing or being complacent. Having parked up and putting the bike onto the stand, the candidate will be invited into the test centre for test result, feedback and paperwork.

To leave the Motorcycle Manoeuvring Area:

- ▶ Select 1st gear and carry out rear observations
- ▶ When the gate is open, ride forward and out of the test centre
- ▶ Park as instructed by the examiner or in a safe place
- ▶ Stop, select neutral and put bike on stand
- ▶ Dismount and await further instructions from the examiner

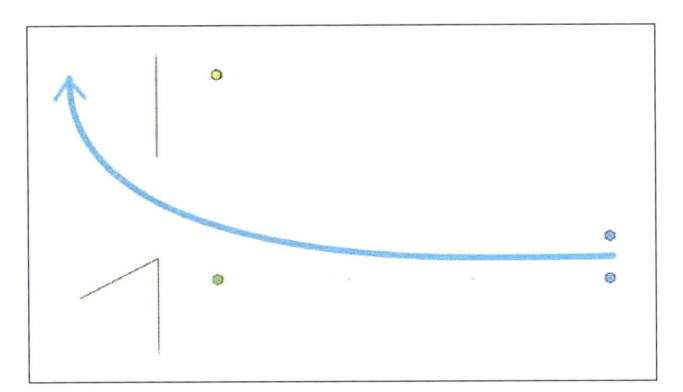

Diagram: Leaving Motorcycle Manoeuvring Area (left circuit)

Instructor Tip

"The test isn't over until the bike is securely on the side stand."

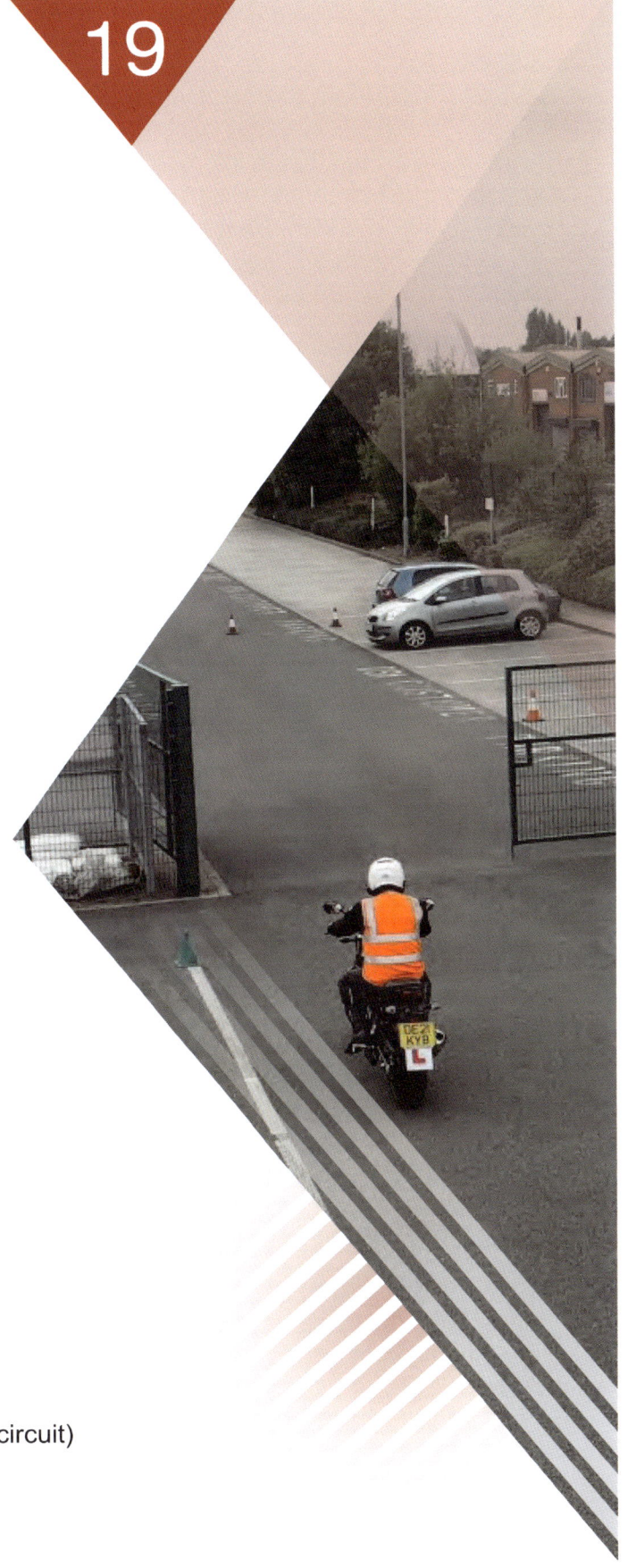

KEEP IT ON THE BLACK STUFF

TAKE RESPONSIBILITY

Riders must accept that to improve their riding skills they must undertake ongoing training, coaching and guidance. Rarely does a rider's perceived ability match their actual ability but many tend to think they are better than they actually are.

The importance of ongoing training is crystal clear to develop personal performance, police riders are at the top of the tree because of training. Be reminded that they once started off as novice riders.

The Module 1 and Module 2 tests are merely stepping stones for the future on two wheels. They are to biking what base camp is to Everest, but to reach a higher position requires time and effort with further enhanced training.

Motorcycle training schools will be able to guide riders on the best advanced training routes. They will advise new riders on the Enhanced Rider Scheme (ERS), which is run by Driver and Vehicle Standards Agency (DVSA) instructors.

Advanced rider qualifications can then be taken through organisations such as The Royal Society for the Prevention of Accidents (RoSPA) and the Institute of Advanced Motorists (IAM).

Riders must always take responsibility for their own riding and always be committed to ongoing training and development. The most common error is when riders think that once they have passed their test, there is nothing more to learn. Experimenting by trial and error is not the best course of action to take, it usually ends in disaster!

If it is accepted that as riders, safety is always in your own hands, you should improve slowly into a more proficient and capable rider. The hope and aim for Motorcycle Riders Hub is that all new riders have the ability to **Keep it on the black stuff**

KEEP IT ON THE BLACK STUFF

NOW FOR MODULE 2

Once the Module 1 test has been passed it is time for the Module 2 test. Because it is a two part practical motorcycle test, both tests must be passed within two years of the motorcycle theory test certificate being issued.

During the Module 2 test, the examiner will follow on their motorbike during a road based assessment to ensure the candidate has the required road skills.

Test routes cover a variety of road and traffic situations, including an independent ride. The Module 2 test generally takes around 40 minutes to complete, even though 57 minutes are allocated.

Candidates should book their Module 2 test through a professional motorcycle training school to ensure they get the best support in order to pass. Having sufficient training will give candidates the highest chance of passing the test first time.

Taking a DIY approach for the Module 2 test is not recommended. Candidates who are not properly prepared are more likely to fail their test and require further training to ensure they are ready, resulting in it costing more because of lack of training and a longer waiting time to take another test.

Motorcycle Riders Hub advice is to always prepare properly and be mentally ready before taking a Module 2 test.

KEEP IT ON THE BLACK STUFF

Printed in Great Britain
by Amazon